FRONTISPIECE

"IF YOU ARE NOT AFRAID TO LOOK BACK, IT MEANS THAT NOTHING YOU ARE FACING CAN FRIGHTEN YOU."

James Baldwin

ENDORSEMENTS

"The pride which the Boley sanctuary afforded a black man to recognize his manhood, and the ambitious dream of a young lad fulfilled, is a story that is worthy of being passed on to present and future generations."

Victoria A. Banks
Guidance Administrator
Detroit, Michigan Public Schools

The first edition of this book: "High Noon At The Boley Corral" was awarded by the State of Michigan "Special Tribute" award, Feb. 19, 1984. State representative Teola Hunter presented the award for "Literary Contributions to the history of Black Americans."

Teola Hunter,
Michigan State Representative

HIDDEN HEROES ON THE CHECKERBOARD PLAINS

(THE ALL-BLACK TOWN TERMINATED REIGN OF NOTORIOUS BANK BANDITS)

Printed in the United States of America

ISBN #0-9634727-0-4
Library of Congress #81-114028

An Autobiographic Documentary
Published by Diversified Publishers, Inc.
246 Maddison Ave., Suite 324
Detroit, MI 48226
Second Edition of the revised first edition:
"High Noon At The Boley Corral"
Copyrighted in 1981

TONY BROWN'S COMMENT

A BOOK REVIEW

Did you know that on Thanksgiving Eve, November 23, 1932, "Pretty Boy" Floyd's notorious gang attempted to rob the Farmers and Merchant Bank at Boley, Oklahoma?

If Alex Haley's "Roots" turned the spotlight on truth in Afro-American history, "High Noon At The Boley Corral" finally turns the spotlight on deception, (by omission) about one covered-up Black town that destroyed the nationally-famous, bank robbing, "Pretty Boy" Floyd gang.

The author grew up in Boley, the largest of several all-Black towns that sprang up around the turn of the century in what was still known as Indian Territory. Blacks were denied residency in White communities. However, the towns became landmarks of self-sufficiency.

Although there is a demand for his information, the black entrepreneur must become the catalyst, as Smith has. He has "discovered" America's history for us. We must, in turn, discover Smith, if the circle is to be closed.

WM. JUAN ROBERTS
(Designer of books front cover)

The truth Versus...
THE "PRETTY BOY" MYTH

Two movies have been made from stories about the life and times of Charles A. "Pretty Boy" Floyd, bank-robbing terror of Oklahoma in the early depression years. The most recent film was shown as a T. V. Special in the spring of 1974.

Both films conveniently omitted or refused to give proper credit to those responsible for Floyd's gang being captured or killed in the all-black, Oklahoma town of Boley. Neither film mentioned any of the details of how and why, after three years of successful bank "banditry", his career in Oklahoma ended at Boley. Neither film mentioned that the black bank president at Boley, who pulled the bank's alarm, facing the bandits, was killed by George Birdwell, Pretty Boy Floyd's fiery lieutenant, reputedly the "brains" of the gang. Both films also omitted mentioning a young Black man, Charles Glass, who accompanied the gang and was gunned down along with Birdwell by Boley lawmen and the town's vigilantes.

Among the primary objectives sought in this documented story is to report historical facts, pertinent to Blacks in complementary roles in history, who have been skirted, or purposely omitted.

Sequences in this documentary describing the attempted raid on the Boley Bank have been expressed in my earlier book, Boley's Gold. The registered copyright number is A770728. (August 9, 1976)

AUTHOR'S NOTE
(Acknowledgments)

Much of the background material for the bank robbery by the Pretty Boy Floyd's gang was secured from the Oklahoma Historical Society, Oklahoma City, Oklahoma.

The list of those persons who have extended me courtesies in this endeavor is extremely long. Whereas some may be missing from the list, I offer my sincerest appreciation for their encouragement and help.

At Boley, my warmest thanks go to the following Boley residents interviewed: Mr. and Ms. Exodus Adams, Langston McCormick (former Boley sheriff, during the Pretty Boy Floyd era), Letish Watkins, C. J. Moon, Sr., Lilliard G. Ashley, Sr., and his wife Velma, Millard Brooks, Sr., and Millard, Jr., Abigail McCormick (widow of Herbert C. McCormick, bank bookkeeper who shot and killed Pretty Boy Floyd's henchman, George Birdwell in the 1932 bank robbery) Mrs. Kissie Robinson, Sandy Clark, Mrs. Donnie Mae Lawson, Ms. S. M. McThonican, M. H. Martin Jr. (Detroit), Harrell King (Oklahoma City, Okla.), and Sylvester Shanks (Boley, Okla.).

At Earlsboro, Oklahoma, I wish to thank Dock Hearn and Melvin Logan. Two former residents of

Earlsboro, now residing in Detroit are: William T. McKenzie and his brother Alonzo McKenzie. Also at Detroit: Ms. Elizabeth Hood, Ph.D., Rev. Nicholas Hood, John Frazier, Dorsey Walker, Ph.D., Dr. J. A. U. Carter and my wife for everything positive.... plus.

Last, but not least, I wish to thank my seven older sisters and brothers. They are Ms. Luada Oliver, Washington D.C., Ms. Ruth Bunkley, Denison, Texas; Ms. Esther Spillman, Chicago Ill.; Ms. Naomi Mims, Huntsville, Ala.; Mssrs. Homer, Nathaniel and Cornel Smith, all of Detroit, Michigan.

For special historical research, much credit goes to the son of my former English instructor at Wiley College, Dr. Arthur L. Tolson. (His father was Dr. Melvin B. Tolson). Arthur Tolson's book, The Black Oklahomans, 1541 - 1972 was highly informative.

Other sources of references include The All - Negro Society in Oklahoma, by Mozell Hill. The Longest Way Home, by William. E. Bittle and Gilbert Geis, published by the Wayne State University Press.

Detroit, Michigan, June 14,1976

DEDICATION

The following true story is dedicated to those Black pioneering Oklahomans, living or dead, who espoused the Boley Dream - participating in its brief years of fulfillment; thereby capturing the illusive bird of freedom, while most of Black America could only watch the bird in flight.

ROUTE TO BOLEY, OKLAHOMA

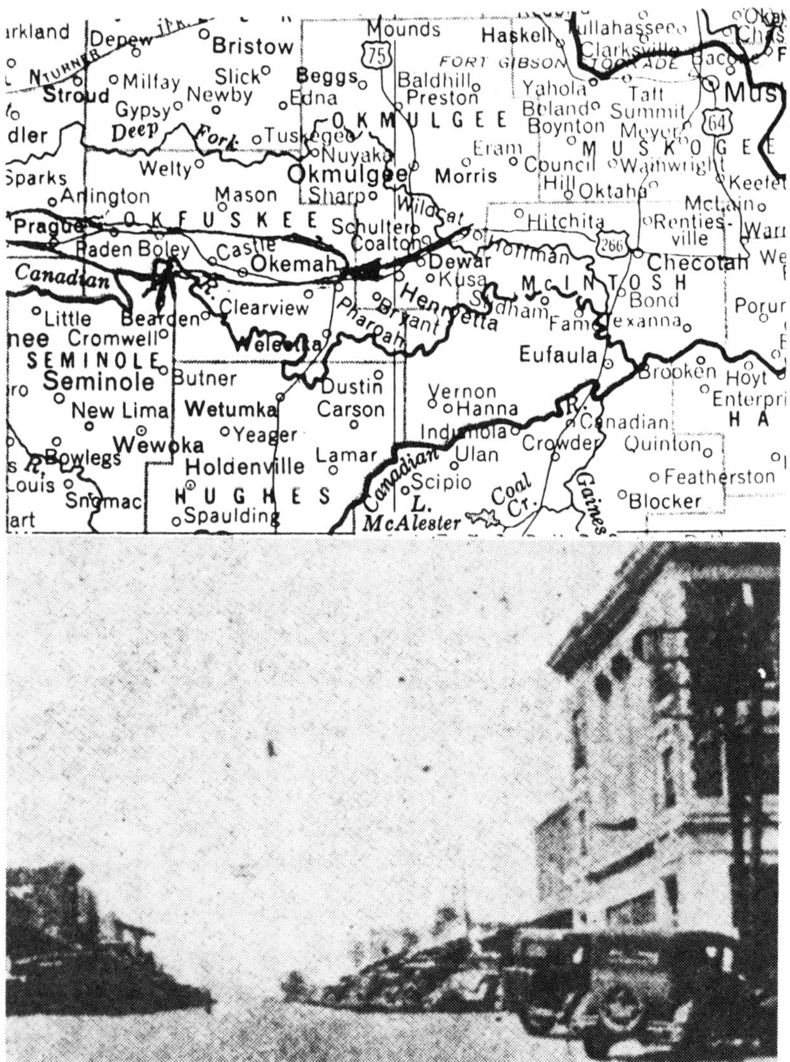

Main Street, 1932

TABLE OF CONTENTS

CHAPTER 1

PROLOGUE
"Return to Boley"– My hometown

My eyes feasted on the rolling blackjack hills, dotted with tangerine-colored puddles and ponds. We were driving through that Red Beds area in my home state, where the red clay tints the standing waters in colors near to its own. The Spring rains from the night before left splashes of the brilliant color all along the super-highway between Spencer and Prague, Oklahoma. The picturesque scenery made William King's pick-up truck glide like I was still flying in the big airliner that had taken me to Oklahoma City the day before. My destination was Boley, Oklahoma–my home town.

William King, a life-long friend, who lived on his ranch at Spencer, had picked me up at the airport. I had spent half the afternoon and the following Thursday night as a guest in his home.

After rising early the next morning and consuming a sumptuous country breakfast, we were off to our hometown, Boley–known at one time as the "largest, most progressive, all-black metropolis in the world." In 1975, it was celebrating its 70th anniversary.

When I informed William and his gracious

wife that I was writing a book about our home town, their Southwest hospitality expanded even further. Their two votes to drive me the forty miles to Boley won out over my gentlemanly dissent.

Within an hour, William and I were passing the vacant lot on Boley's main (Pecan) street, where the King family's ice plant had stood for nearly a half a century. Over the years, Boley sports fans deduced that the five King brothers gained their superiority in athletics through the extra muscles they'd developed at Papa King's ice house. Clifford "Shorty" King will long be remembered for his sensational backfield running at Langston University during the mid-thirties.

I had planned to arrive at Boley a day ahead of the crowds that would be arriving there for it's 70th Anniversary celebration. Flip Wilson, the renown comedian had agreed to lead the big parade down Boley's main street. My reservation had been made for a room in the home of Ms. Bennie Dolphin, affectionately known as Sister Bennie. Sister Bennie was an amiable, gray-haired former secretary and relative of Boley's late Dr. W .L. Paxton. I hadn't seen my hostess since my Boley High School days, (1933).

Tomorrow, I thought, the streets will be filled with lots of folks I haven't seen since I was a teenager. Flip Wilson and his camera crew were scheduled to film the gala week-end festivities, which climaxed with the annual county-wide rodeo. Flip had shipped his special van, with the camera equipment, all the way from Los Angeles, California.

Boley's 70th Anniversary Committee members were euphoric about their success at securing Flip to participate in the celebration. For his efforts, the City officials were to make him Boley's honorary sheriff. Flip later cracked that he "enjoyed the job because there was no crime at Boley." Flip's film (not video tape) covered the highlights of various events that would be included in the famed comedian's TV series "Travels with Flip" in October 1975.

It was sundown, Friday night. I sat on Sister Bennie's porch and watched the creeping darkness slowly devour the straggling beams of sunlight. My hostess introduced her second guest, who had just arrived from Oklahoma City. Just minutes later, Sister Bennie announced that *supper* was being served. It was the first time I'd heard the word *supper* in many years. I was elated to hear it. I wouldn't have to be standing in line to buy the bar-be-que on Main Street.

I sat on the porch wondering if I would have any luck meeting Flip Wilson. Late that afternoon I'd discovered Flip had arrived at the Holiday Inn Motor Lodge at Shawnee, Oklahoma. He and his crew had made their headquarters forty miles south of Boley.

My primary motive for making the trek to Boley this year was to meet and present Flip Wilson with my freshly penned historical novel–set in Boley's boom days. Without a rent-a-car this time, I resigned myself to relax and take my chances on catching up with the creator of "Geraldine."

As early as nine o'clock Saturday morning, some of Boley's early-birds were searching for and claiming their parade viewing spots on main street. First come, first seated was the rule. Except for the noticeable absence of booze and drugs, the crowds were pouring in, like the hippies of the sixties converging on that era's mammoth rock concerts.

The motorcycle caravans soon began to roar up and down Main Street. The two-wheeled juggernauts of noise quieted down only after the street was closed to all traffic, except Flip Wilson's big station wagon and super van.

By parade time, the rain threats were over and the sun came burning through the clouds, as if it had been ordered to do so. Flip Wilson was the Grand Marshal, leading the parade. He was attired in a gold and silver cowboy outfit, riding a white horse. His hat was banded with rhinestones, matching the rhinestones on his holster and boots. The thrilled female fans screamed and swooned as Flip waved out kisses.

Oklahoma's governor followed behind Flip in the parade that lasted nearly an hour. While meandering in the crowd, meeting folks and watching the parade, I learned that I could see Flip at the banquet that was to be given in his honor on Sunday afternoon.

When nightfall came to Boley Saturday night, approximately thirteen thousand Boley visitors and returnees turned the town into a boom town once again. Because the rodeo was usually jointly sponsored by Boley and Okemah, the county seat, the police force had been integrated. They were beautiful; so were the crowds.

For fear of being crushed by the crowds at the rodeo, I took a rain check and returned early to Sister Bennie Dolphin's hospitality. My parents had been close friends of the Dolphins long before I was born. It was only natural that my conversation with my hostess would dwell on incidents and events of the past. The treasure that is to be found in older people is that they are the living witnesses of the past. When they're gone, their testimony becomes hearsay information, unless it is recorded.

In 1969, retired Sheriff Langston McCormick had recorded, (on my tape recorder) how Sister Bennie was delighted to hear that my book carried her story. I was happy to be able to double check what I had written, though five years late.

Early Sunday afternoon, I began to walk rather casually across Main Street towards the Boley High School assembly hall. The five unpaved street blocks stretched out before me; one block was up-hill. I stopped for a second to lean on my walking cane and rest. There were no moving vehicles on my street as I looked ahead down the stretch of red clay road. As I glanced behind me, a car turned off Main Street in my direction . The driver drew closer. I was unable to recognize him. He stopped and asked if I needed a lift. The good Lord will answer prayers, I thought-even before you ask Him-sometimes.

Naturally, I was elated to get a ride. I wouldn't have been able to walk the distance he finally took me. Moreover, the miracle was, that of the thousands of cars still in Boley, my driver was a seventy-year-old Bolyite named Boley Spears. I remember that there was a man named after Boley. My brother, named Nathaniel, had told me the story often enough.

In 1905, the year my father settled at Boley, the swaddling, all-Black town was celebrating its first anniversary. A campaign was announced in conjunction with the birthday celebration. The first baby, (male) born in that year was to be awarded the name Boley – to honor and cherish for the rest of his life.

It was a thrill to be sitting beside this copper-colored, spry, seventy-year-old Boley Spears. My brother had been born the same year, (1905) missing the name and the honor by only a few weeks. However, Nathaniel was a blunt and extremely frank person. He commented the following about Boley: "They couldn't have tagged that name on me with a hammer."

Even as I was finally being introduced to Flip Wilson, I was apprehensive about the manuscript I was about to give him. Its title was "The Checkerboard Sea." It was all fiction; my town's name was Promiseville and the owner of Boley's bank was named Thompson, instead of Turner.

When I arrived at Flip's banquet, Mayor Theodore McCormick had already pinned the honorary sheriff's badge on the smiling comic's lapel. I did, however, witness Flip Wilson presenting the town his check for $5.000 to buy a new sheriff's car. He left an indelible impression on everyone as jester, humanitarian and special human being, he could stand a few lessons in horseback riding.

As I deplaned at the Metropolitan Airport in Detroit, I felt that my trip had not been in vain. Next, I would write a true story about my unique hometown. In that story I would document the last attempted bank robbery by the Pretty Boy Floyd's gang in Oklahoma. It happened in my home town.

During my three day stay in Boley in 1975, one of the founders, or very early settlers spoke to me about a movie that he had seen about Pretty Boy Floyd. The film told the story of the notorious outlaw, glossing over the facts about how his career in Oklahoma was ended at Boley. This film is still a popular late night rerun on television

On March 22, 1979, I had the opportunity to view parts of the film. In relating how George Birdwell, Pretty Boy Floyd's lieutenant, was killed, Pretty Boy's movie distorted the facts beyond all belief. I was shocked and mad.

The movie portrayed Pretty Boy's girlfriend, or wife, reading about Birdwell's death in the newspaper. She read from the phony newspaper these words: "He was shot to death at the Boley Trucking Company."

Today, the town of Boley still lies almost secluded, off old Highway '62. The new East-West super highway might have followed the route of '62, but it skirts Boley by approximately four miles to the south.

Each May 30th, thousands of Boley old-timers and their descendants still, religiously make the pilgrimage back to Boley, where they know the Pretty Boy Floyd's gang met its Waterloo. During the Decoration Day weekend, the featured rodeo, the parade and other special festivities capture most of the huge throng that chokes its narrow streets. But most of the permanent residents, many of whom are elderly and retired, proudly sit on their porches, eagerly receiving this annual booster injection of pride and nostalgia. Unlike the "old soldiers" that General Douglas McArthur referred to that "never die, but just fade away", Boley lives on, and its history refuses to fade away.

Note: The name 'Oklahoma' is from the Choctaw Indian tribe; meaning "Home of the Red man"

CHAPTER 2
"BLACK-HOMA" ROOTS

The year was 1932. Our nation was caught up in a live or die struggle with the great depression. Small towns like Boley were rapidly being deserted as money-less, jobless ghost town.. The key contributor to most of the violence inflicted upon Oklahoma's small towns was a trio of bank-robbing bandits called the Pretty Boy Floyd gang.

During The first eight months of 1932, Floyd's gang robbed over thirty-four town banks in central Oklahoma–averaging a bank a week. The majority of those thirty-four robberies were achieved without firing a shot. Some town's sheriffs reportedly conveniently left the towns, (went fishing) on the day the Floyd gang announced its intentions to rob their respective town's bank.

I was a teenage farm boy, living on a farm near Boley on that historic day of the demise of the gang at Boley. Boley was the largest of the remaining all-Black towns, (an endangered species variety) left over from the Indian Territory days.

Booker T. Washington, the renown educator and founder of Tuskegee Institute, was highly impressed with his visit to the all-Black towns in the Indian Territory when he visited them in 1905. Years later, he reported on his visit, paying a special tribute to Boley, Indian Territory.

Excerpts from:
"BOLEY, A NEGRO TOWN
IN THE WEST"
By: Booker T. Washington

"In 1905, when I visited Indian Territory, Boley was little more than a name. It was started in 1903. At the present time it is a thriving town of 2,500 inhabitants, with two banks, two cotton gins, a newspaper, a hotel, and a 'college,' (the Creek-Seminole College and Agricultural Institute.)

Boley, although built on a railway, is still on the edge of civilization. You can still hear on summer nights, I am told, the wild notes of the Indian drums and the shrill cries of the Indian dancers among the hills beyond the settlement.

Mr. D. J. Turner, who owns a drugstore and has an interest in Farmer's and Merchants Bank, came to Indian Territory as a boy, and has grown up among the Indians, to whom he is in a certain way, related, since he married an Indian girl, and in that way got a section of land.

I learned upon inquiry that there was a considerable number of communities throughout the Territory where an effort had been made to exclude Negro settlers. To this, the Negroes had replied by starting other communities in which no white man was allowed to live. But among these various communities there was one of which I heard more than the others. This was the town of Boley, where, it is said: "No white man has ever let the sun go down upon him." (End of quote.)

(From LOOKOUT Magazine, Vol. 88, P. 28).

The same year Booker T. Washington arrived at Boley, the new town's newspaper, The Boley Progress, devoted a large section of its first issue to advertisement - extolling the great opportunities in the newly-incorporated town. A portion of that first printing read as follows:

> SITUATED ON THE FORTY SMITH AND WESTERN RAILROAD ABOUT...
> SEVENTY MILES EAST OF GUTHRIE, OKLAHOMA AND... TWELVE MILES FORM THE OKLAHOMA
> TERRITORY LINE IS THE CHARMING AND THRIVING LITTLE TOWN OF BOLEY.
> IT IS SITUATED IN A BELT OF FERTILE LAND THAT IS WELL ADAPTED FOR AGRICULTURAL PURPOSES.

COTTON, CORN, WHEAT, OATS, AND POTATOES PRODUCE ABUNDANTLY. GREAT OPPORTUNITIES AWAIT THE COLORED PEOPLE HERE; WHERE THEIR CHILDREN CAN **EDUCATE** AND **FIND OPPORTUNITIES TO EDUCATE SAME.** THERE ARE TWENTY THOUSAND ACRES OF LAND, THE FINEST IN THE CREEK NATION, SURROUNDING BOLEY TO BE LEASED AND BOUGHT BY NEGROES.

My parents could not resist the following, rather quaint poem about the new, black boom town. Papa's cousin, named Higgenbotthams, who was already settled at Boley, promptly mailed him this poetic masterpiece. It reads as follows:

Say, have you heard the story
  Of a little colored town
Way over in the nation
  On such a lovely sloping ground?
With as pretty little houses
  As you ever chance to meet,
With not a thing but colored folks
  A standing in the streets.
Oh, 'tis a pretty country
  And the Negroes own it too
With not a single white man here
  To tell us what to do–in Boley.

And I will tell that fellow
Whoeer he may be:
If you don't think we are colored
Just come here and see.
Get on the 'Fort Smith and Western'
The train will bring you here;
Take any of the coaches–
You have no cause to fear.
Here, a Negro makes your dresses
And a Negro makes your pants
And hands out your mail
If you'll give him half a chance–in Boley.

Signed, Uncle Jessie

The "five civilized tribes" had been forced out of the deep South, (1838). They were the Cherokee, Creek, Seminole, Choctaw and Chickasaw. They were given rights to all of present-day Oklahoma, except the panhandle. Each of the five tribes formed a nation. By treaties, the United States promised the Indian nations, and guaranteed that the Indians would own their land: "as long as grass shall grow and rivers run." Each Indian nation established its own legislature, courts and written laws, and built its own capitol. For fifty years, the general westward movement passed by the Indian Territory and these so-called "five civilized tribes."

The new hope of freedom on this prairie promised-land, just prior to statehood in 1907, was like a breath of fresh air; especially for the black pioneers. Although the climate was hot and arid, and the land composed mostly of a shallow top soil, it was land! It was land that was either free, or you could buy it 'dirt cheap' and call it your own.

The new black landowners were mostly ex-sharecroppers. They knew how to raise cotton. Here, they would be on their own.

A county -wide, political power center, Boley was Number One among the twenty-seven Black towns. It soon earned recognition throughout Oklahoma –as the nucleus of Black pride and self-sufficiency.

The Black settlers, like D. J. Turner, (the president of Boley's bank in 1932) and my father were among as esoteric a group of pioneers that ever set foot in that vast Southwest wilderness. Many of these settlers, (blacks and whites) were to be the recipients of free land. With proof of residency on an Indian chieftain's land for six months or more, prior to 1907, they were entitled to one hundred and sixty acres of free land. The proposal of Sojourner Truth to the U. S. Congress for "forty acres and a mule" became a reality forty years later in the Indian Territory.

Unforgettable acts of containment through the state's Grandfather Clause, the threats and the two

Klan lynchings. In 1911, a Boley resident, Laura Nelson and her son had impacted greatly, in terms of unity of defense against all predators. Even in the midst of the great depression, the central feeling among Boleyikes was that:

"Their town was their castle."

My father's roots extended deep into the Indian Territory's young history of unlimited freedom. He had migrated there from Texas in 1899. That was the year of Papa's first big "step in the dark"–as he called it.

My mother and father, with their three children, had traveled in a covered wagon train with four other black families. They crossed the Red River over the Texas border near Denison, Texas.

As a child, I was thrilled by tales of my parents fording rivers and living in tents for over two years. The family settled first at the prairie village of Shawnee, Indian Territory.

In 1898, the year before Papa's wagon train arrived at Shawnee, the territorial governor had threatened to send the militia into that area–Pottawatomie County. Rioting between whites and blacks was rampant. At Norman, I. T., twenty miles west of Shawnee, all blacks were forcibly banished from the town.

It was in such a climate of hostility that the migratory blacks soon began to establish their first all-black enclaves. Edwin C. McCabe, a former black state auditor from the state of Kansas had already established the all-black town of Langston, I. T., (1890).

Contrary to the Indians, these black pioneers were homesteaders. They were ready to fight for their rightful piece of the territorial pie. If they were not accepted in the white settlements, they were determined to live exclusively outside of them–building their own towns.

Fortunately, the Indian Territory, that had been given by treaty to the *Five Civilized Indian Tribes*, was located outside the purview of the federal government's jurisdiction. Indians and black freedmen (some former slaves) had lived together since 1844–in harmony. The black freedmen had frequently intermarried with their former Indian masters–especially the Creek Indians.

The sixty acres of land purchased by the Fort Smith and Western Railroad's town-site company for my home town's land-site was purchased from a freed-man's daughter. Her name was Abigail Barnett.

Several years later, she married a young Boley pioneer, named Herbert C. McCormick.

Almost thirty years later (1932) this same Herbert C. McCormick worked as a bookkeeper in Boley's Farmers and Merchants Bank. He emerged as a Boley hero in that shoot-out with the Floyd's gang.

Just two years before my father arrived at Boley (1903) with his five children, the Fort Smith and Western railroad line, already under construction, was to slash its way through part of our future farm. Its route cut a path from the Oklahoma-Arkansas state border to the territory's capitol, Guthrie, Oklahoma.

There were two work gangs building this railroad line through that virgin wilderness. One gang was white, the other black. Each of the two crews had been forged into highly competitive teams. At times, the sound of hammer on steel was so loud that the mythical "John Henry" might have surely stirred in his grave.

The Fort Smith and Western officials had been highly successful in their "separate, but equal" system of railroad construction. At nightfall, the biracial crews bedded down in their tents in separate work camps along the railroad's right-of-way. The black work gangs had black foremen and black subcontractors; the white gangs worked under white supervisors.

The wooden cross-ties were cut from the indigenous post oak trees, but the men who skillfully laid them on the railroad bed were mainly migratory workers, nursing a hope to make this new territory their home.

The small village of Weleetka, Oklahoma was a temporary headquarters of the officials of the railroad. An official named Lake Moore was particularly impressed with the miles of railroad track laid by the black work gangs. He was prompted to speak to another railroad official about an idea he had that was almost revolutionary at that time. His idea was to construct a railroad depot and watering tower, where blacks might use them as a nucleus to build an all-black town. Lake Moore believed blacks could manage the railroads depot as well as whites–if they were given a chance.

Although the officials who were first approached by Mr. Moore thought differently about his idea, the top railroad heads agreed with him. B. T. Boley was one of these officials. They named their town after him. The Fort Smith and Western railroad built their depot and water tower at Boley, Indian Territory.

CHAPTER 3
Growing up in Boley

Nineteen-thirty-two was destined to be the final year that prohibition would prevail as the law of our land. Prohibiting the sale of hard liquor in public places via the *18th Amendment* was now doomed to be repealed in 1933. Moreover, the big bootleggers in Oklahoma were expanding their operations. The word was out that Oklahoma and several other southern states would remain "dry" states, in spite of the new impending national decree.

Although Oklahoma was now nationally famous for its 'black gold', (crude oil) another potent liquid called bootleg whiskey was already a flourishing business. John Dillinger, Pretty Boy Floyd and John Q. Public had been influenced by the proliferation of the evils of their times. Successful bootleggers and bank bandits alike were rapidly becoming heroes to the hungry and down-trodden.

Charles Pete Glass, a local unemployed, black gambler had spent most of his twenty-six years in and out of Earlsboro, Oklahoma. Glass knew George Birdwell's family; they were neighbors. He couldn't resist Birdwell's invitation to join the Floyd's gang. Birdwell, sometimes called "The Hatchet Man," had been Pretty Boy Floyd's ace lieutenant since the gang began terrorizing Oklahoma in 1930. Before the depression, Birdwell and Floyd had worked as laborers in the oil fields at Earlsboro, and nearby Seminole. Bradley Floyd, Pretty Boy's brother, also lived in the Earlsboro area in 1932.

Among my most noteworthy achievements in 1932, as a junior at Boley High School, was my appointment by Mr. Herbert C. McCormick, as assistant superintendent of the Boley's Antioch Baptist Church. Mr. McCormick was the bookkeeper at Boley's bank. D. J. Turner, the president of the bank, was Mr. McCormick's employer, and also a deacon at Antioch.

During 1932, each of these men was to make news for the New York Times, and the front page of the Daily Oklahoman.

I recall the financial strain that my parents had endured, when Papa paid fifteen dollars for his contribution the church's building fund. The tidy sum, during that depression year, went toward the purchase of one stained glass window for the new church. My father would have been happier, if he could have been able to contribute more to building the new brick edifice on Boley's north end.

My mother was admittedly more dedicated to saving her pennies than giving to the church. Thrift hitched itself to her shadow. She had given deacon Colonel Smith and all of her eleven children to the

Baptist Church. None of her brood ever left home on Sunday morning without their coins for the church collection.

Although Mama occasionally accentuated her distinguished, mixed grey hair beauty by dressing up on Sunday, she left the church predominantly to Colonel.

H. C. McCormick's decision to appoint me his assistant in his Sunday School could have been based on his knowledge that my Papa had high hopes for me being a Baptist preacher. Mr. McCormick and my father knew that I was literally the last chance, (of the six Smith boys) for one to carry the word of Jesus to the fallen, wherever they might be.... if only I could hear my 'calling'...

The 'calling' that I was listening to in the summer of '32 was not to be a preacher nor a Pretty Boy Floyd. I just wanted to save enough tuition money to attend Wiley College, at Marshall, Texas by 1933. My idol, a former Boley High basketball star named E. B. Cavil, had just returned to Boley, after playing on Wiley's championship team. He was now a coach, back where he'd starred on THE BOLEY BEARS' state championship basketball team in 1928.

The year 1930 hangs out in my memory like a huge neon sign. Mama could no longer resist the temptation of reuniting with seven of her eleven children way up in Detroit, Michigan. Besides, Papa was finally heeding the good news he'd heard about a manufacturer named Henry Ford, who was paying black workers five dollars a day to work in his automobile plant. Since his prostate operation had almost healed, he figured he'd give that Ford fellow a hand, and maybe spend his declining years with his boys. One of his five sons, Homer, had built a successful business up there in Michigan.

Papa was confronted with the task of running his farm with one teenage son and a slightly retarded daughter, who had suffered from a thyroid condition. Besides, in 1930, the living reality that engulfed us at Boley spelled depression, as clearly as ROLAID spells Rolaid.

The American economy had struck a 'dry hole' and thousands in Oklahoma were beginning to feel the results of the 'crash' on Wall Street the year before. Earlier in 1930, Pretty Boy Floyd had begun his program of robbing 'the rich' that ran the banks in Oklahoma.

I certainly didn't want to leave Boley and the now practically new inside gymnasium and basketball court at Boley High. I have no doubt that the departure of Papa's children up North and the subsequent depression prices for cotton challenged his Christian principles, based on the Bible, especially the twenty-third Psalms: "The Lord is my shepherd, I shall not want. He maketh me to lie down in green pastures..." However, if this prairie-promised land had temporarily eluded him, he would do as he had done in the past–move on to the greener pastures.

By late summer of 1930, everything in our house had been sold. Toby and Rhody, our sixteen hands-high Missouri mules, and all of our stock were also sold. The house and the farm were rented out. Renting instead of selling proved to be Papa's smartest move.

CHAPTER 4
"A Taste of "Up North"

Winter came in Detroit much sooner than was accustomed for the last of the late arriving Smith clan. I remember the heaping piles of white snow that stood in rows along Forest Avenue, blocking my path to Northeastern High School on Grandy Street. I could never understand why the white students didn't catch cold without anything on their heads in that cold winter weather. For many, the constant accumulation of snow flakes in their hair were their only caps.

I soon discovered that blacks didn't play on the basketball team. I didn't quite understand why. In my classrooms, white faces rowed up beside me in formations, like live snow-men–strangely cold. I had never sat in white classes before.

I surprised myself and everybody else by being the first to find the unfindable, a job in depressioned Detroit. I was hired as an apprentice shoe shine boy.

When I wasn't getting into mischief, like hitching a ride on the back of the St. Antoine Street trolley car, I found myself watching the diminutive black shoe shine ace, Jimmie Jones. Jimmie Jones' small cubical for doctoring shoes was jammed in between my brother, Homer's restaurant and his two-flat, where we lived on Forest Avenue. Jimmie may have been the best shoe shine man in all Detroit. At least, I wasn't the only one who thought so. Many of his customers were celebrities–musicians who played in the sensational McKinley Cotton Pickers' band. They were being featured at the fabulous Graystone Gardens on Woodward Avenue, not far from the parlor. Their favorite 'open all night' eatery was "Smith's Cafe and Sandwich Shop."

I didn't work up to be good enough, as little Jimmie's protege, to shine band celebrities' shoes. The singing star in the band, Fat Head Thomas, was one of Jimmie's best customers, along with Dave Wilburn, guitarist and Claude Jones, trombone player, who was from Boley.

I wasn't allowed to touch Jimmie's big tipping customers, but split the ten cents charge for regular shoes with Jimmie. I kept my tips!

I never learned to pop the shining rags like Jimmie Jones, but I did learn to put my best effort into getting that perfect gloss on people's shoes and smile–with the outstretched hand for that tip. At Jimmie's shoe shine parlor, Papa's famous axiom became crystal clear; "Anything worth doing is worth doing right."

Three months passed and Papa still refused to believe that Henry Ford's town didn't have even a porter's job that wasn't filled. He began to realize that his fifty dollars deposited on an apartment would soon be lost; if he couldn't find a job.

Many of the long wintry nights in Detroit found more members of the Smith's family together than had been the case for many years. Such gatherings offered idle time to talk about the "good old days" back at Boley. Suddenly, the talk of the "good old days" turned to talk about the new days of one Pretty Boy Floyd. It was late January, 1931, when we first learned, via the grapevine, about an Oklahoma bank robbing bandit named Pretty Boy Floyd. On January 14, the Floyd gang had robbed the First State Bank of Castle, Oklahoma, which was only six miles from Boley.

Papa's concern about a job grew less, as his new anxiety over friends at Boley and its bank began to steal his thoughts. D. J. Turner, Papa's friend and president of the Farmers and Merchants Bank at Boley had vowed to defend the town's savings at all cost.

The possibility of an assault on the town of Papa's roots by the rampaging Floyd gang added fuel to the flame of homesickness, already burning in Papa's heart. Without his stock to look after, or fences to build, or fertilizer to spread on his tiring land, he lived in a prison of loneliness–next door to despair. However, his wife Hager, and the majority of his family were near him. Listening to them talking about old times made him forget about hard times–the present.

Deep down inside, my Papa wasn't worried about Pretty Boy Floyd, as long as sheriff Langston McCormick and retired sheriff John Owens were still in Boley. Papa agreed that Owens was one of Boley's baddest sheriffs–if not the baddest.

He always wore a big black cowboy hat, with a bullet hole through its crown. I learned that he earned that bullet hole while barely escaping death in a shoot-out with a band of bank robbers in the early twenties. The gang, known as the Haskell Gang, had robbed the bank at Prague, fourteen miles from Boley.

As stories of the Floyd gang continued to emerge up North in Henry Ford's town, more speculations were expressed about who would capture him and get the $6,000.00 reward. For reasons that Papa couldn't really understand, some friends of his in Oklahoma gave him the nickname Robin Hood–"The Sage Brush Robin Hood."

After one year at Northeastern High in Detroit, Michigan, we returned home to a state that was being dubbed the "Dust Bowl" and "Pretty Boy Territory." And Boley sat slap-dab in the middle of it.

CHAPTER 5

Pretty Boy Floyd...

"Robin Hood of the West?"

Blind Pigs, as they were called, fostered much prostitution, bootlegging and gambling and provided a convenient meeting place for bank robbers. Each of this quartet of illegal bed-fellows had pipe lines of communication with crooked cops and corrupt politicians. Racial barriers fall easily in such an environment. A short time after the Floyd gang had predicted the robbery, they successfully robbed the banks at Paden and Prague, Oklahoma, in one day. Pete Glass was summoned by Birdwell to appear at the "Floyd house", the gang's hideout. It was located approximately twenty-five miles south of Earlsboro, deep in the Cookson Hills.

The Cookson Hills country was a well-known sanctuary for gangsters, dating back to the post civil war era and the legendary Jesse James. Birdwell's reputation as the "brains" and "trigger man" of the gang was common knowledge to lawmen in Oklahoma. C. A. Burns of the State Bureau of Criminal Investigation stated the following about Birdwell; "Birdwell was the man who planned their activities and handled their machine gun in their raids."

Birdwell was stockily built, ruddy complexioned man. His hair was dark and stubby, displaying a wave almost as short as his temper.

Charlie Glass held no particular allegiance for my home town, Boley: for its state-wide popularity or its well-earned recognition for black achievement and race pride. Glass had been reared on Turkey Creek, just north of Earlsboro.

Self-identification for Glass was reasonably more difficult to achieve than for most blacks in that neck of the woods. Many of his childhood playmates had been poor whites and Indians. At this juncture in Glass's maturation period, Boley was perceived as just another town where he applied his expertise as a gambler on Saturday nights. As far as Boley's viability or extinction was concerned, Glass could care less. Except for the money in Turner's bank, the whole town could roll up in a cotton sack and die. He needed Boley's endowed ethnocentricism like a snake needed hips.

Pretty Boy Floyd's boasting about his prediction to rob Paden and Prague was like Mohammed Ali, calling the round in which his fights would end. What was even more gratifying to Pretty Boy's supporters was, like Mohammed Ali, he did it. And his Okie friends cheered. The Boley Okies refused to join his fan club.

The Daily Oklahoman, the state's biggest newspaper, with home offices in Oklahoma City, had covered the doublebank robbery made by Pretty Boy's gang. Their daring feats had been accomplished almost within gun-shot of Boley, without firing a shot.

Pete Glass was highly impressed at what he had read in the papers. Consequently, Birdwell had little or no resistance from the young ambitious Glass, when he was offered the chance to climb up into the big, big time. Now, Birdwell would have to convince Pretty Boy that drafting Pete Glass and choosing the Boley bank as a target were expedient or wise moves.

The same "Daily Oklahoman" newspaper that carried the details of the twin robberies by Pretty Boy also listed some facts that the neophyte gambler, Glass, was interested in. One fact was that during the first three months of '32 the banks in Oklahoma had given up over $62,000 to bank robbers–nearly all of it to Pretty Boy Floyd's gang. As a consequence, the Oklahoma Bankers Association had offered a

$5,000.00 reward on Pretty Boy's head – dead or alive. The state offered another $1,000.00.

Pete Glass had heard about the nine or more killings that Pretty Boy had been given credit for. He didn't know that Pretty Boy and Birdwell were near to the breaking point in their relationship. A salient point in Pretty Boy's list of complaints was Birdwell's too-often over-indulgence in drinking whiskey. His warnings to Birdwell were to no avail. Pretty Boy was looking for a new lieutenant.

One must assume that Birdwell was envious, if not jealous of Pretty Boy's widespread publicity, while he, "the brains" of the outfit, remained an unsung nobody in the gang.

During the late summer of 1932, Pete Glass stood before Pretty Boy at the gang's hideout, deep in the Cookson hills. A rash of fear, filtered with excitement, must have chained Glass' thoughts to Pretty Boy's alleged killing record, listed in the Daily Oklahoman newspaper. The bandit's resumé on the front page dated back to 1925. Most Robin Hood-type bandits historically seldom killed maliciously, even when pushed in self-defense of their mythical hero image. The clean-shaven, somewhat handsome Pretty Boy must have brought a montage of mixed images to the hopeful apprentice, Pete Glass.

Jesse James, reportedly, never robbed a preacher, a widow, an orphan or an ex-confederate of the Civil War.

Bringing this young Negro to Floyd's hideout wasn't amusing to the Sage Brush Robin Hood. Floyd had warned his side-kick about too much drinking too many times before. In fact, he had just recently made an appointment to talk with an old acquaintance from the East named Adam Richetti, who had just been paroled from the prison at McCalister, Oklahoma. Oklahoma banks had been picked pretty clean and the lure of Chicago and the Al Capone territory, without Birdwell had begun to concern Pretty Boy. Richetti was his connection with the Chicago syndicate.

The following dialogue is offered as dramatization of what transpired at Pete Glass' first confrontation with Pretty Boy.

Glass broke a breathless silence and proceeded to qualify himself for being at the hideout of the handsome twenty-five year old bank robber, who was already a legend.

"How'd you like to take on the biggest colored bank in the country?", asked Glass. "You talking about Boley , boy?" Pretty Boy questioned.

"That's right," Pete replied.

"Off-hand, I'd say nix on that idea," Pretty Boy informed him.

"You liable to get 'yo' tit in a ringer foolin' with them Boley boys. I wouldn't be' fur' it... I reckin' I'd be specially against trying to knock over them, seeing that nigras ain't got but that one bank in this state. That mean they ain't gonna give it up, without somebody dying... I don't want no part of that nigra town or its bank!"

Pretty Boy was preparing to depart their scene, when Birdwell, having lost some stature before his new recruit, interceded to persuade Pretty Boy to listen to Pete's story.

"Now it won't take a minute, big man," Birdwell argued, "Go ahead, Pete, you tell 'em bout my plan!"

Pete Glass reluctantly began to speak. "Well they's some friends of mine up there at Boley. I believe we...er...could surprise em–me chaufferin' the car could fool 'em. I been there lots of times."

Pretty Boy looked briefly at the door, then back at the light-skinned Pete Glass. He shook his head and walked out of the room in disgust. What would his partner stoop to next, he thought.

Pete Glass probably complained that the' terror of the plains' just didn't think a Negro had guts enough to rob a bank–just enough guts to steal chickens or watermelons. He'd show him.

Pete Glass, George Birdwell and the third man, C. C. Patterson, drank a toast to their impending success at the fat black bank at Boley. The three of them would bring in a gusher at Boley. Pretty Boy's abstaining made it that many less to split the take with.

On May 2, 1932, Al Capone, gangland's number one kingpin was sentenced by a Federal Court to eleven years at the new Federal prison on Alcatraz Island. Hundreds of hero-worshippers had waited outside the Illinois Courthouse in Chicago to cheer him. Though he was handcuffed and completely surrounded by F.B.I. men, he told reporters at the scene: "I'm a saint to these people."

The acceptance and support of Al Capone and Pretty Boy Floyd by thousands of depression-whipped Americans is explained by psychologists as an expression of anti-establishment.

If Pretty Boy was to be true to his Robin Hood guns, Boley might not have been considered by him as a part of the ruling establishment; the big city banking institutions that were foreclosing on his poor Okie farming friends. Pretty Boy's coolness toward robbing the Boley bank could be perceived as positive evidence that his Robin Hood image included some empathy for all of the depression poor-including some blacks that he knew.

CHAPTER 6
A Wolf at our Door

The busy east-west Highway '62 skirts the south-end of Boley, and continues west for sixty-five miles. There at Oklahoma City, it intersects the famous route '66. Main Street in Boley empties into Highway '62 and dead-ends there. From this dead-end, looking north up Main Street, the entire business district of Boley (in 1932) rises plainly in view.

Should you walk the five blocks of paved sidewalks, going north, you would pass through the heart of Boley; its two-story department store, its bank, the three story Masonic Temple Lodge Hall, an electric power plant, an ice factory, a soda pop factory and three cotton gins, down near the railroad tracks and depot.

A shallow creek runs a snake pattern alongside the railroad. During the hot, dry, summer days this shallow stream is barely a trickle, except for the "Round Hole" swimming retreat, a quarter of a mile east of town. Excluding the worst of droughts, the "Round Hole", shaded by huge willows, supplies most of the swimming thrills for the 'town boys' all summer long.

For my father, Colonel Smith, the stingy creek had served a different purpose. In the early spring, the heavy spasmodic rains swell the narrow creek's channel, inundating the bridges along High '62 – near our farm. When this happened, numerous new horseless carriages got stuck in the mud. Papa was always ready with his huge, sixteen hands-high team of Missouri mules to rescue them. The extra money from pulling the cars out of the mud came in handy, especially in those lean years, when the boll weevils plagued the cotton; that staple crop of all Oklahoma dirt farmers. In 1932, most of them survived about like papa - barely making 'buckle and tongue meet.'

Our house and farm that we returned to that year had been very well taken care of while we were getting a taste of up-North. By the summer of '31, we were settled back into the farming groove.

Black-topped highway '62, that cut its route in front of our house was to carry grim reminders of the debilitating effects of our state's dust storms. Hordes of westward bound Okies, fleeing their farms in the flat plains areas passed our house each day. Jalopies of every description chugged along, perilously overloaded, headed toward highway '66 at Oklahoma City. There, at the state capitol, they took the famous route '66– a direct route to the golden orange groves of sunny California.

The fruit growers needed pickers, and these uprooted, hard working, Okie farmers were looking for any kind of job. John Steinbeck wrote about them in his famous novel, "The Grapes of Wrath." His words were: "Some were paid off with a pound of flour and a spoon of lard."

Although the Sahara-like climate had caused Oklahoma, Texas and Arkansas to be declared disaster states, the blackjack hills areas around Boley were less affected. The popular cowboy comedian, Will Rogers, was appointed by the Red Cross to head the fund-raising drive for the three states. The new, well-earned name for Oklahoma was the 'Dust Bowl.'

With volcanic fury, the scorching winds had sucked away the land's over-dried layer of top soil and blown it to the skies with a pale amber glow – like some ominous gases, belched from the sun's boiling cauldron of fires.

While the Sooner state trembled under the torture of the dust and the depression, Pretty Boy Floyd's gang continued socking it to the banks – mostly in the small towns. The FBI dubbed him 'Public Enemy No. 1.'

In March 1931, Charles A "Pretty Boy" Floyd, alias Frank Mitchell or Pretty Boy Smith, robbed the Bank of Earlsboro, practically at his own back door. On July 1st. his charm worked again at the Commercial State Bank of Bristow. Boley sat between these two deflated oil-boom towns of Bristow to the north and Earlsboro, eight miles to the south.

Shortly after our return to Boley, we heard that Pretty Boy had established a good rapport with a few black Okies, as well as white ones. If any poor black farmers were hiding out anything more profitable than boot-leg whiskey, it was Pretty Boy. In times of crisis, the "huddled masses' of the poor and hungry don't have time to question the source of the free "bread."

By early spring of 1932, my Papa was making a desperate effort to convert his cotton farm into a small dairy and truck farm. Boley still didn't have any soup lines like Detroit, and Papa was bent on keeping it that way. He had an obsession about growing foodstuffs and peddling it to the neighboring old boom towns that were weathering the depression's storm.

By summer of 1932, after some financial help from his sons, especially Homer, the Detroit restaurateur, our barnyard began to fill up with livestock. Papa purchased the purebred Jersey cows for butterfat and Holsteins for quantity sweetmilk.

My mother ordered her first hundred white leghorn baby chicks and an oil burning brooder from Des Moines, Iowa. The brooder kept the baby chicks warm, like a mother hen; until they were old enough to scratch for themselves. I remember rats killed nearly half of them in one night.

Papa took on a drifter for a hired hand at thirty dollars a month, plus room and board. He made the third man in our house, including myself.

The wolf wasn't heard to howl as loudly at our house as he howled at some around Boley. We sold blackberries, grapes and peaches from a small stand, erected alongside the highway. By mid-summer, when the sizable crop of watermelons and cantaloupes were ripe, Papa and I started trucking. We trucked the double-bedded wagon loads of Irish-grey watermelons and cantaloupes to towns as far as we could travel to and from in one day.

My ubiquitous teenage chores had stretched into twelve and fourteen hours of hard labor. Yet, I seemed to thrive on the new diversified tasks, especially the long wagon trips across county lines. I developed a companionship with my father that I had not experienced before. He was in his early sixties, but still could jump and click his heels together three times in mid-air, better than I could.

I soon forgot my shoe-shining days up in Detroit and the race to Warfield Theatre on Hastings Street every Saturday night. Moreover, certain memories clung on fingertips in my brain. Drugstore buddies, like Crit McSwain, Randall Hall, Leonard Andrews, John Frazier, Oscar Solomon, Alex Smith and the neighborhood Breau Brummelites' club ceased to haunt me. Yet, the unpleasant incidents, like the time we were refused service at the White Tower hamburger place on Woodward at Forest, lingered on among the guarded corridors of my mind.

For the first time in my life I began to realize what the town of my birth, the Boley sanctuary, was all about. It was the one place where a black man was in charge of his manhood. The hamburgers at Baker Roberts' cafe on Boley's main street were twice as good as those at the White Tower up in Detroit.

A section of wooded land located approximately a mile north of our farm had been abandoned to lay fallow. The deserted pasture, even in normal years, produced only a scattering of blackjack and hickory trees , with little grass between the trees. Like the summer of '31, the drought of '32 had burned out the grass in this pasture, leaving a young, iron-gray colt to nearly starve. I had spotted the skinny razor-backed colt several mornings, straining his neck through the pasture's barbed wire fence enclosure. He was trying to reach the skimpy patches of green grass alongside the section line road.

Each morning, during the hot summer dry spells, I herded Papa's small herd of milk cows along this road where the starving colt was imprisoned. On this morning I herded our cows past this abandoned pasture–slowly moving north toward the open grazing ranges on a grassy hillside. By noon, the herd's bellies were filled to bursting, looking like moving rain barrels on four legs. The grazing finished, I would drive the cows back home to our small sudan grass pasture already eaten clean by the herd. They remained there until milking time.

Every day, as I passed the wooded pasture, I began looking for the starving colt. One day in early August, as I returned from grazing our herd, I decided to go after the young grey horse somebody was neglecting or maybe had run away and got trapped in the grassless pasture. I deducted that after a few weeks' diet of hard corn and tender loving care, he would be mine–all mine.

The day I lassoed the colt, I named him Po Boy. It was noon and I hurriedly pushed our milk cows and yearlings back home. I was anxious to show off our new barnyard addition.

Mama wasn't too impressed with the puny Po Boy and continued with her churning on the back porch. It was dinner time. The sturdy, two-gallon hand churn, with which my mother used to turn sweet cream into butter, was suddenly heavy to turn. The butter had congealed, just in time for my dinner.

"It's almost ready," Mama called out. "You can have fresh butter with your ho-cake bread."

"Pork an'beans...Sho' smells good. I'll wait for the butter," I answered, with relish.

Mama was busy setting my dinner out on the kitchen table, when a truck pulled off the highway onto the section line road in front of the house.

"Mama, here come some Okies!" I yelled. "Want water, I guess."

I began talking on an old subject, as I walked

into the kitchen. "You know what mama, the next time one of them rubbernecks calls you Auntie, I'm gonna say, "Hey, man, how can she be your auntie, unless we are cousins?"

"Now you stop that, Leon!" Mama retorted, ceasing to pat and mold the fresh butter. She continued, "The Lord has blessed us with a well... pretty as a fountain, between two white rocks. Folks got to have water and Okies are folks... too. They goin' a long way through that desert and all. We got some poor land here, and it takes a lot of patience. But you know what? I'd rather be a 'Auntie' than an Okie!" she smiled.

A tall, lean, sunburned man, in baggy, frayed blue overalls was facing me, when I stepped from the back porch to the graveled backyard. A gaunt, blue-eyed little girl held onto the tall man's hand, standing slightly behind him.

"Mornin' yo all," the straw-hatted Okie whined. "We be clear runned out of water. Sho' be obliged to use yo' well."

Suddenly, Mama was answering the stranger through the open screen door. "You're welcome to all you need!"

Leaving the well, I watched the poor uprooted, itinerant farmer carry the two jugs of water toward his overtaxed, overloaded old truck. Three flaxen haired children peeped from behind the canvas covering.

He was carrying all of his worldly possessions in that jalopy. He cranked the motor and the whole truck began to shimmy. Undauntedly, the tall depression casualty stepped to the brief running board and slid under the steering wheel.

Mama and I watched and waved as the struggling old truck passed on the highway. The children waved back at us. A weather beaten, hand scrawled sign flopped back and forth from the back end of the truck. It read: "California or Bust."

Henry Marriott, our mailman, passed, returning from his mail deliveries. He waved and I went out to fetch the mail from the mailbox. We subscribed to the Daily Okemah Ledger newspaper. I was reading it aloud when I returned to the back porch.

"Floyd gang runs amuck in the eastern part of the state. Notorious bank robber on spree again. Commonly known as the Sagebrush Robin Hood, Charles A "Pretty Boy" Floyd staged a daring robbery of.... " I stopped and turned toward Mama.

"You believe that 'bout him giving money to the poor, Mama?" I asked.

"Well, I heard he gave out some Christmas baskets–paid for 'em or something in some little old town." Mama continued to clean the dishes off the table as she talked. There was always something that kept her hundred and fifteen pounds moving. She continued with a bit of information that shocked me.

"I heard somebody say that he hides out with colored sometime."

I was forced to laugh and said something like, "I betcha he'd never be caught hidin' out round Boley."

The lunch for Papa and the hired hand was packed and ready for me to carry to the alfalfa patch where they were baling hay. With a tin pail in each hand, I walked leisurely across the terraced, sloping acres, wondering how long Pretty Boy would last up in Detroit, Michigan.

I walked past the orchard and across the terraced, sloping field. I could see Papa pulling the big rake over the freshly cut alfalfa hay.

Minutes later, back in front of the house on the highway, a sleek, black touring car grounded to a halt on the graveled soft shoulder. Mama was watching the two men in white sailor hats looking cautiously at her house as they approached the south gate at the highway entrance to the yard. She hoped they would be looking for peaches. They could see some of the heavily loaded peach trees from the highway. The two men walked gingerly up the graveled path to the back porch. By this time, Mama's hopes had fallen. She saw the steam oozing up from the dusty hood of their parked car. One of the men was tall, with an athletic build. The second man was much shorter. His hair was dark and he wore a thin moustache. They just wanted some water, Mama thought. She was searching her porch for a suitable bucket, even before the tall man spoke. One man remained in the driver's seat of the car.

"We'd be obliged to use your well, mam, car's runnin' hot."

"Jes' help yo' self," Mama replied pleasantly. "One thing we got is plenty of water."

"You wouldn't happen to have a bucket we could borrow, would you?" the clean-cut pinkish tan man asked.

She handed him a two-gallon bucket. He passed the bucket on to the shorter man, making conversation as his companion walked briskly towards the well.

"Plenty hot!" the tall, city slicker -type stranger intoned.

"Mam, you got a mighty good smell comin' from yo' kitchen. If I wasn't so hungry I wouldn't have the gall to suspect you'd sell a mess uv' it. I ain't clos't to beggin,' but that smell's makin' my mouth run water."

Mama was stunned at the polite, talking man. And before she could close her mouth, he had pushed a green bill through the partly-open crack in the screen door.

"I 'spect I could spare a mess or two, maybe for all that money," she replied. "Lord, you wait right there." Mama pushed the bill down into her bosom too quickly to see its denomination. Off she went into the kitchen. "I'll throw in some corn bread, I jus' cooked it!"

Mama filled a quart jar full of navy beans with a hunk of salt pork on top. She put a large piece of corn bread in a paper sack and was back at the door in no time. By the time she was handing the tall man his vittles, the shorter one was returning the bucket he used to put water in the car. She watched the two men walking past her honeysuckle bush at the gate. She was out of breath and relieved when she heard the car groan and saw the dust rise up from the soft shoulder of the highway. She sat down on the chair near her churn on the porch and reached down under her dress collar at her bosom. She fingered the bill. She unfolded it and looked at it, casually. She screamed. It was a twenty dollar bill! She jumped from her chair talking to herself, "Lord will answer prayer!"

"Lord – let me go call em!"

She grabbed her big sun bonnet and raced toward the field where her men were working. She had gotten past the orchard when she realized it was getting near to the hottest part of the day.

"Leon!" she called, using all of the wind in her lungs. She called the second time, waving for one of us to come to the house. I dropped my pitch fork and started to trot up the inclining slopes– recently terraced to hold back the top soil, according to C. E. Johnson, our country farm agent.

"I'm coming!" I yelled back at Mama.

Walking back to the house, Mama's mind began to function more normally. She thought about the newspaper and Pretty Boy Floyd.

When she reached the house she went directly to the phone. She reached for the receiver, then changed her mind. I was at the door.

"They're might near 'ta Paden by now-anyway," she mumbled. "Those men, that were here, I think they were Pretty Boy's gang," she shouted. "...And look, the big one, look what he gave me. Twenty dollars! All I did was give 'em a mess of them beans in a mason jar, and one of 'em put water in their car!"

I inspected the bill briefly. I took Mama by the shoulders and guided her to a chair at the kitchen table.

"Here, yu' sit down," I told her. "Wait till I tell about this! You know what Mama? They pointin' at the Turner's bank, I bet. That mean one, Birdwell, they say he carries a machine gun. I was thinkin' about an idea when you called. That sho' would a been something, if I had uv' been here and could uv' trapped that gang of Pretty Boy's."

"Leon, it's hotter then I thought," Mama replied. “Maybe the heat’s done got to your common sense. Talkin ‘bout trapping Pretty Boy. That man may hand out twenty dollar bills here and there, but he hands out bullets a whole lot faster.”

“Mama, when we were up in Detroit, I shined a guy’s shoes who said he worked as a bell hop at the Detroiter Hotel. It was right downtown on Woodward Avenue. It was a hangin’ out place for the ‘Purple’ gang, he told me. They were mostly in bootleggin’ whiskey, the protection game, an’ so on.”

“The Purple gang? You shore that heat didn’t get to you today? I never heard a no Purple gang, Lord!”

“That was their name, alright. He said he used to get big tips from ‘em sometime–not no twenty dollars, though. I reckon I could have been finishing Northeastern High next year... if Papa hadn’t a took and brought us back to Boley. But that’s okay; I’m still goin’ to college.”

“We sho’ are beholden’ to you for–comin’ back I mean. Well, yo Papa sho’ nough needed you on this farm. But you gonna go to college, if I have a say so about it. This twenty is goin in a special piggie bank, as a starter.”

Mama realized that I wasn’t in love with the farm or Boley either. However, I didn’t hate it with a passion, like her other sons did. Maybe they didn’t have a horse like my Po Boy.

CHAPTER 8
Thanks for 'Schoolin' Land

By the middle of my second year back on the farm, I began to realize that Boley was something special. My parents and the other settlers who had put their roots down there were neither separatists nor nationalists –like Marcus Garvey or and Chief Sam. They were merely trying to live out their dreams that would not be deferred again in this former free land–the Indians' former happy hunting ground. They had compromised between a prairie panacea and the new Oklahoma's bi-racial, segregated towns. They would keep their minuscule black kingdoms–defending them against all predators, especially Pretty Boy.

The year we returned from our disappointing ten-month visit to Detroit, Papa had put ten of the best acres of our forty-acre farm in alfalfa. Alfalfa, it seems made the best kind of hay for Papa's milk cows. The alfalfa hay bales were the primary food for our small herd during the winter season. I remember the sweet smell of alfalfa after the bales were stacked high in the loft of our barn.

In the spring of 1932, my parents had given me approximately two acres of land for the expressed purpose of raising cotton on it. It was designated as "schoolin" land. My obligation was to break the ground in Spring, plant the cotton seeds, weed the young cotton-plants and cultivate them to the best of my cotton-picking ability, all by myself. I cared for it like it was a prospective gold mine. By harvest time, the yield was expected to be at least one bale of cotton. Cotton was the pre-depression money crop of most black farmers in Oklahoma.

It was a breezy, late September Sunday afternoon. The customary routine for the family was to sit on our front porch, digesting the Sunday dinner, and watch the cars sail by. The conversation had wandered from Amos and Andy to Will Rogers. Without the laughs form Amos and Andy, the homespun humor of Will Rogers and the advent of Franklin D. Roosevelt, Papa might surely have been looking for another 'Chief Sam' movement back to Africa.

My precious cotton patch had turned into a sea of pearly white, in spite of the near-drought weather conditions. The day grew nearer when I, with Papa at my side, would ride into town together, atop our wagon with triple sideboards bulging high– full of the white stuff that would be turned into my tuition money at Wiley College.

Among the many islands of gratification that loom forever in view from the farmer's vantage point, in his veritable sea of troubles, is his constant role of being a shepherd. Not only is he the shepherd over his animals, his living plants that he grows for survival, but he is master and head physician over fruit trees, the fish in the pond, the young heifer with calf and the mare carrying her foal. It is care and guardianship over such a domain that lifts his spirit, especially when nature unleashes her cruel tormentors. So much so was Papa's subconscious filled and attached to the living things outside his house, often times Mama felt neglected. From such a feeling of exclusion she would frequently say, categorically, "Yo Papa thinks more of his stock than he does me."

Papa answered philosophically, "Stock is like money in the bank; the more you put into them, the more you get back."

Over the years, before the depression, I'd gone to the cotton gins and watched the farmers with wagon loads of raw cotton being sucked up from their wagons by the huge vacuum hoses, and marveled at the seed-stripping operation. At one time our town had five cotton gins in operation.

I shall never forget the fall of '32, as the Summer's oven closed its doors and Autumn's cooling breezes rushed in. Over the years I had seen the droughts that seared the crops like a flame, drying up every watering hole–leaving not even a mud catfish or a tadpole alive. I knew of the devastation when the tiny boll weevil had prevailed upon Oklahoma's cotton farmers. However, Mother Nature waited until my cotton patch was ripe for picking, then released her cotton -killing tormentors with a crash of thunderbolts.

Later on, during another Sunday afternoon in September, I was dribbling my basketball on the worn down stubble of brown grass in our front yard. Suddenly, after a few practice shots at the makeshift basket, I noticed a boiling mass of black clouds. I stopped my practicing and hurried toward the back porch. I threw my ball inside, on the floor of our screened back porch. My yellow and brown dog, Ponto, sensing the weather and time of day, quickly vacated his lair under the porch and tore out in front of me for the barn. Ponto was halfway to the cow pasture, when I mounted Po Boy and galloped out the barnyard gate after him. My heels dug into Po Boy's flanks. Within minutes, I was tight in behind our herd of cattle, pushing them home.

A few minutes later, the thunder was rumbling at synchronized intervals, like an approaching beast, gaining on its quarry.

Mama had already joined the beehive of activity that a threatening tornado creates. The windows must be quickly checked and secured, the rain barrels set properly at the corners of the house to catch rain water. Her apron will be used to gather the egg. Then, using her free hand, she will snatch the few bed clothes left on the clothes line to sun.

Soon, the rat-a-tat sound of hail on the roof of the house brought words of speculation from Papa that it wasn't a tornado on the prowl. It was a hail storm.

"Hail don't run with no tornado," he said, somewhat relieved. No one went to the cellar.

The next hour seemed like a lifetime. I'd never seen such a sight before. Hail, hail, hail as big as billiard balls bounced and rolled; piled up against the fences surrounding the back yard. The whole house seemed to be the target of some siege from above. Howling winds, carrying warheads of ice from Mother Nature's arsenal had attacked, battering down the small limbs from the black locust trees that bordered our lawn. The attack was like a billion golf balls sprayed from the mouth of God. The intermittent thunder calls could barely be heard over the prevailing assault.

"Lord ha' mercy!" somebody spoke. "That stuff could kill a horse."

Suddenly, the winds hushed and a scattering of small marble-sized hail stones bounced and danced on the white carpet of hail. Then suddenly, it was as quiet as a tomb. And the thunder growled.

By nightfall, the winds had taken their leave. Although the misty drizzle of wetness lulled our house in a peaceful, nocturnal hypnotism, no one seemed able to sleep through the night.

By five o'clock Mama was up as usual, fixing the breakfast. A symphony of sounds could now be heard from the hen house, with roosters crowing, leading the serenade to the new day. Papa and I surveyed the damage done to the barnyard and orchard areas. Water in the horse lot stood up to the horses' fetlocks. We sloshed through a sea of hail-picked green apples in the orchard and feared to go near the cotton fields.

Papa began to console me by quoting his favorite simile: "Farming is like taking a step in the dark."

At the breakfast table, Papa began with his usual lengthy prayer. He always began with: "Numberless, merciful, heavenly Father..."

Even in the darkest hours, his faith glowed through the darkness like gold. The gold in the faith was surely Papa's true "black gold." This morning, it will sustain him, as it had done so many times before. That tiny mustard seed of faith spoken of in the Bible, had been firmly implanted in the souls of most cotton farmers like Papa. So, they left the miracle of good harvest in the hands of the Lord. Prayer was the bulwark of their hopes - the vitalizing song of their souls.

My hopes of tuition money from my cotton had gone down with the hail. However, next Spring, when the mustard plants in Mama's garden bust forth in their brilliant, canary yellow blossoms, I shall once again eat the delicious green mustard leaves. I would not know it is called "Soul" food. However, I'm sure I shall get out Papa's turning plow and turn up the fresh damp earth and once again plant another cotton patch, for my tuition, (schoolin') money.

CHAPTER 8
All Eyes on the Prize!

In late November, the first chilling signs of Winter came whistling boldly across Boley's black-jack and hickory hills. These early, gale-like winds were called Northers. In '32, the Northers brought record cold, adding more misery to the poor, particularly in the bigger cities. At Oklahoma City, over 15,000 breadwinners were still looking for jobs–many searching the garbage cans for food.

Franklin Delanor Roosevelt had sailed into the White House with an over-whelming landslide victory for the Democratic Party. His silver-tongued oratory had captured the votes of millions of bankrupt Americans–whites and blacks alike. The single, upsetting factor that reaped the landslide victory for the former New York governor was the millions of newly converted black Democratic voters.

In Detroit, they were honoring an outstanding black native son, named Eddie Tolan. The former great Detroit high school speedster had won two gold medals at the 1932 Olympics in California.

Keeping a watchful eye on the school of my choice, Wiley College, I learned that it too had won an outstanding victory in world forensic competition. The Wiley varsity debate team, under the direction of Melvin B. Tolson, had just won over Oxford University's debate team at Oxford, England.

Papa held onto hopes that the Depression would send one of his prodigal sons home. But I knew that would never happen. Any one of them would rather be a lamp post in Detroit than the Mayor of Boley.

Meanwhile, on the day before Thanksgiving Eve, Pretty Boy's lieutenant, George Birdwell, C. C. Patterson and the new black recruit, Pete Glass, were busy plotting and planning their raid on the Boley bank. During that afternoon, the trio passed our house, headed for Boley to double-check Glass' information about the layout of the town. They picked Horace Aldridge's pool hall as their vantage point to watch the activity at Mr. Turner's bank.

From the pool hall, diagonally across the street from the bank, they played pool and cased the traffic in and out of the bank. A Boley old-timer named Sandy Clark played pool with them, unaware of the true objective of their presence.

Upon leaving, not one of the three strangers in the car suspected they had aroused any suspicion while at Boley. They were wrong!

An attractive young secretary named Bennie Dolphin, who worked in Dr. W. A. Paxton's office reported having seen the car to Sheriff Langston

McCormick. Someone in the car had made flirting remarks as they passed her on Main Street. She thought the occupants of the car looked suspicious.

During the early evening hours that followed, Birdwell, Patterson and Glass proceeded to get drunk together. They spent several hours at one of Pete Glass' sister's house near Earlsboro. While there, Pete bragged to his sister about the gang's plans at Boley. He boasted how he was "going to show the gang how to rob a colored bank."

Early the next morning, Thanksgiving Eve, (the day of the attempted robbery) the three bandits ate breakfast at Earlsboro, at the house of a black neighbor of Birdwell's named Dock Hearn, Sr. Hearn's home was located less than a mile from where Birdwell lived with his four children.

Dock Hearn was a special friend of Pretty Boy Floyd. Hearn reveled in the fact that Pretty Boy had given him a 'bo' silver dollar for every bank he'd robbed in Oklahoma. Dock Hearn didn't try to hide his clandestine association with the indigenous Pretty Boy, who had brought fame to Earlsboro and Cookson Hills area.

While Pretty Boy Floyd was hiding out with blacks like Dock Hearn, he had learned about the Boley breed. He didn't want any part of D. J. Turner's bank. If George Birdwell would not heed Pretty Boy's advice to by-pass Boley, the stubborn little lieutenant might get caught like General Custer in his last stand at Little Big Horn.

CHAPTER 9

"A Town United"

The Farmers and Merchants Bank at Boley held mortgages on many of the farms in the outlying neighborhoods. However, the oppressive act of foreclosure on the Boleyike farmers was seldom executed, during the early depression years.

D. J. Turner, like the rest of the bank's stockholders, was also a merchant. Turner had great respect and leniency for his impoverish, victimized brothers, who were caught in the Depression's wake. No one that we knew was thrown out of their homes, like many farmers were in other counties. It was for this reason, above all others, that the Boley bank was a focal point of pride, rather than the source of all evil that plagued the state's farmers. Papa and Mr. Turner were friends for over thirty-three years. They had been neighbors back at Shawnee, in 1899.

The last thing that Papa wanted to do was to ask his boys up in Detroit for more money. However, the bottom had dropped out of the cotton market.

What little we had barely paid the hired hand. As Papa would say later: "...We were hard-pressed to make buckle and tongue meet." He decided to go see his friend, Dave Turner at the Farmers and Merchants Bank.

The front door of the Farmers and Merchants Bank opened at the southeast corner of the one story, brick building. Diagonally across from the bank on the northeast corner, the stately Masonic Temple, (Mason's lodge) building towered three stories above the forty-odd stores on Main Street. Facing the lodge hall and adjacent to the bank, on the north was Bill Hazel's two-story department store.

D. J. Turner met my father just inside of the bank and escorted him to a partitioned section behind the teller's window, through the swinging, waist high doors.

"You're looking like a picture of health, Brother Smith," Turner began, "How's the missus?"

"Oh, she's jes fine, D. J. I'm still the worse off," Papa replied.

After a brief conversation about the predicament of the state's farmers and the nation as a whole, Papa reached the point regarding his rather unusual visit. He wanted to borrow two hundred dollars, using our forty acre farm as collateral.

Papa should have realized that friendship was one thing, business was another. Turner answered Papa's loan request by explaining that there wasn't a bank in the whole state that would loan cash secured by cotton farming land. Most of the Okies that passed our house, going to California, were from farms that had been foreclosed on.

The one thing that disturbed Papa in his interview with Turner was that a bootlegger could borrow money for a whiskey still quicker than he could,

D. J. Turner, president of Boley's bank

Herbert C. McCormick, Bank Cashier

putting up his land for collateral.

Papa also learned first hand, that the bank was counting on its new alarm system to help apprehend Pretty Boy, should he pay it a visit. When activated, the bank's alarm alerted four other stores on Main Street. The alarm was triggered by lifting the last dollar bills from the teller's cash box connecting the two electrodes wired there. The four other stores were electrically wired to the bank. Papa had reason to fear for his church brother and friend of thirty years. Turner would be the most likely one to pull the alarm in a bank robber's face.

Among those stores that had the extension alarm installed were: Bill Hazel's department store, Shorty Bragg's barber shop, Horace Aldridge's pool hall and John Owens's meat market. The number one Boley vigilante chosen to respond to a possible robbery alert was John Owen, Boley's retired town marshal, who ran a butcher shop on Main Street.

It was Thanksgiving Eve. D. J. Turner sat at his large dining room table sipping his hot coffee and peering across his living room through the opening of the tied-back velvet drapes that were draped in front of his bay windows. His eyes seemed glued to the red clay patch of Main Street that awaited his appearance. However, his thoughts were staked out on a different range – a different time frame. It was time for reflecting. His town had been in trouble before, but never this kind of threat. Pretty Boy had struck too close.

Grace Brock Turner scrutinized her fifty-five year old husband carefully. For breakfast time, he appeared to be carrying an extra heavy burden. She brushed back her long black tresses near her temples and adjusted the plaited chignon ball at the back of her head. Her dark soulful eyes looked up in silence and waited, as a servant awaits his master's voice. If it was something really important, D. J. would discuss it with her, she thought. She was his second wife. Their romance had started while she worked as a pharmacist in Mr. Turner's drugstore. The torrid romance between Mr. Turner and his winsome, "high yellow" employee was Boley's most popular subject for gossip at the time. It wasn't long after Turner's wife had died, in 1927, that Grace and Joe, (that's what she called him) were married.

At their breakfast table on this Thanksgiving Eve in 1932, Grace Brock Turner was somewhat apprehensive about her husband's unusual serious demeanor. He looked worried.

"Joe, you're not drinkin' your coffee," Grace admonished. "Is something wrong? You've been staring out into Main Street as if it were more than just this unseasonable cold weather out there."

"Well, I'm kinda glad tomorrow is a holiday... I won't have to go down to that trap," Joe informed her, then raised his coffee cup and drained the last drops. He sighed and wiped his heavy black, mustached mouth with his embroidered napkin. "You still brew the best coffee in town, Grace." Turner complemented her, then rose and strode toward the front door, and the small alcove and clothes closet. The large wall clock over the fireplace tolled once, signalling the half-hour. It was nine-thirty; close to "banker's hours" at ten o'clock.

Grace had followed her husband in soft, house slippered steps.

"You'd better wear your coat, Joe," Grace suggested. "By the way, what is this 'trap' business you spoke about?"

"Oh, nothing we can't handle, I reckon," Joe replied, and his wife lifted the heavy Chesterfield coat, with the dark velvet collar and held it out in front of him, enabling Joe to slide his arms into it easily.

"Grace," Turner remarked soberly, "I know that someday I've got to go. I'm not afraid to die."

He was hunching his shoulders, settling into the snugly tailored overcoat as he turned and faced Grace's concerned countenance.

"It ain't nothin' to get alarmed about," Turner recounted. "I was jes thinking that whenever I go, I want you to give me a simple funeral - without the frills. I don't want.... I don't want - don't care to have a lot of fuss and expense, that type of thing."

Grace moved somewhat nervously, but handed him his grey Stetson hat without speaking.

"No solos," the banker continued, "jes the choir to sing one or two of my favorite hymns... maybe, "Jesus, lover of my Soul" or "My faith looks up to Thee."

"Joe, I know your favorite songs. Now, something's worrying you. What trap are you talking about?"

"Oh, er - look, don't you worry none. I guess I was thinkin 'bout you." He bent to kiss her good-bye - opening the front door simultaneously.

Grace forced a smile, releasing his hand as she called out, "I'll bring your lunch - I'm making mince-meat pie - your favorite."

It was customary for D. J. Turner to take his morning constitutionals walking the five long blocks, from his imposing brick and white frame home on Main Street to the Farmers and Merchants Bank.

This morning the chilly north wind teased his coat tail and nudged his steps faster than he'd anticipated. His footsteps easily found the familiar concrete path that he had traveled for so many years. However, his thoughts marched to the rhythm of a distant drummer, a bandit on black Buick wheels, who had gained national fame robbing banks.

Pretty Boy Floyd was born in Georgia - later migrating to Sallisaw, Oklahoma.

D. J. Turner walked, oblivious of the early morning's wintry bite. He barely noticed the larger than usual number of farmers in his town, shopping for Thanksgiving extras for their families and shotgun shells for quail hunting on Thanksgiving.

A proud, but somewhat pious man, Turner was the personification of the hopes and dreams of all the Boley old-timers, who had migrated to this all-black port in a storm. For thirty years he had been its dynamic crusader in the political wars, the civil rights fights. He was truly the heartbeat that pumped out the pride and life blood of the town. If he was then, what else could he do but lay his life on the line? It would not be the bank's alarm he would be activating. It was his town's alarm - an expediency designed to save the town people's only cash savings.

D. J. Turner would spring the "trap" - pull the last dollar bills from the cash register, which would automatically set the alarms screaming at four other stores on Main Street.

As D. J. Turner entered his bank, H. C. McCormick, the bookkeeper, gave him his usual friendly salute. D. J. cheerfully returned his greeting and moved spiritedly toward his desk. He peered through the big plate glass window onto Main Street watching for strange cars. He took a closer look at cars carrying any passenger with lighter complexions than a Creek Indian.

Sheriff Langston McCormick had mentioned to his brother, Herbert, that he might seek safety and good vantage point in the large safe in the back of the bank. The sheriff reminded the bank's bookkeeper to be on his P's and Q's and keep a rifle inside the vault. He knew his brother was a good shooter in a rabbit hunt - even quail. Above all, Sheriff Langston McCormick had great confidence in the bank's community alarm system. Moreover, if the alarm system wasn't enough, his brother, Herbert, could play an important role if he reached the man-sized vault in time.

The innovative chain-like system was certainly not foolproof. The electrical wiring connecting the four stores could be perfect, but it's success would depend on several unpredictable conditions. The single person to be exposed to the most danger would be the person behind the teller's cage, at the time of the robbery. It is obvious that the robber would assume that the person directly in front of him would be responsible for setting off the alarm. Would he retaliate with hot lead, or would he scurry and break for a quick escape? This was the uncontrollable chance the person behind the teller's cage would have to take. D. J. Turner was usually at the teller's window to welcome his friendly home town customers.

At nine forty-five in the morning on November 23, 1932, according to radio station KVOO, Tulsa, the temperature was the coldest on record for that date. The Boley sheriff, Langston McCormick, looking every bit of his six feet seven inches, was making his rounds on a brief inspection of the four stores wired to the bank's alarm system. His first stop was at Bill Hazel's big general store and meat market, located on the northwest corner opposite the bank. Lank, as he was called, wore a chubby tan sheepskin-lined coat over khaki pants, stuffed into his calf high, laced boots. His dark blue and brown plaid shirt was unbuttoned at the collar showing the top of his long-johns. He had been the first Boley law officer to be appointed by the Okfuskee County high sheriff, Sheriff J. Wes Kennedy.

Lank McCormick walked and looked like a hungry, copper colored version of "Hop-a-long" Cassidy or Gary Cooper. A tightly rolled, beige Stetson cowboy hat tilted downward as he entered the two big double doors of Bill Hazel's department store. He strode down the long aisles on slightly oiled, hardwood floors to the forty foot meat counter, at the back of the store.

Hazel had a light tan complexion. He wore a thin slick of black hair, parted to cover his balding, receding hairline. He wore his usual white shirt and black bow tie, with a bibbed white apron. He greeted Lank, moving out in front of the long refrigerated meat counter.

"Mornin' Lank. I was just thinkin' 'bout you. Any new rumors about the Okies' friend, Pretty Boy?"

"Nothin' worth repeatin' Bill," Lank replied. "I jes wanted to gab a bit 'bout that veranda..., upstairs; I got an idea or two.

"Jes follow me. I'll show you up ther," Hazel suggested and led Lank up a short flight of stairs.

At the first landing, one door led to the outside veranda. The other led to a storeroom. The long veranda extended halfway along the side of the sturdy, beige and brown frame building. Bill Hazel's concern for the bank was as great as anyone in town. His savings were there.

"You got that concerned look" Hazel said. "Wish we could station a man up here during banking hours."

"I wish we had the money to, Bill. In case Pretty Boy gits any notions, this here's about the best lookout spot I know. You could sure pick 'em off from up here."

"I'll say one thing, it's better'n out there in the streets," Hazel surmised. "Once I hear that alarm, I'll be at 'em, like a duck on a June bug. Git me a Pretty Boy for breakfast."

Before the crash of 1929, when the Fort Smith and Western Railroad line was carrying thousands of dollars in mail cars, Langston McCormick would earn extra money for himself making the train's run to the Arkansas border. He was hired as an extra income. He could use the reward money on Pretty Boy's head. Moreover, Lank had remained convinced that the Okie Robin Hood wouldn't dare invade his territory. Turner's bank had thrived for nearly thirty years without a single threat from bank robbers.

Although the jobless numbered in the millions, and money was scarce, the hard work never ended for me on the farm. Each morning, before going off to school, at least ten milk cows stood patiently awaiting my "milking" hands; first for feeding them, then milking them. We had no milking machines; all milking was done by hand.

During the hot Summer months, the fresh, sweetmilk had to be kept cooled with the cool water from our well. The ten-gallon cans of milk were half-way submerged into long, wooden troughs of cool water on our screened back porch.

Papa used to say, "An idle mind is the devil's workshop." That never applied to me.

As I reflect upon my high school days at Boley High, the nostalgic memories are dominated completely by my activities in the great outdoors of farm life. Within six weeks, the starving colt that I had rescued from the burned out pasture had been transformed into a handsome, gaited saddle horse. Po Boy was soon broken in to carrying me to basketball practice at night, herding cattle in the blazing sun, or hauling me to see my girlfriend on a Sunday afternoon. Po Boy was my pride and joy.

CHAPTER 10
"The Bank Trap...Ready For P.B.F"

I had circled the date November 23rd. on our almanac calendar that hung on the wall above our kitchen table. That date was Thanksgiving Eve, the day the Boley Bears High School basketball team was scheduled to play at Wewoka, Oklahoma. Under the night coaching by Letchen A. Hill and E. B. Cavil, I had made the traveling seven squad member team... Bravo! In order to have this time off from my after school chores my parents had agreed that I could lose a half day at school on Thanksgiving Eve.

During that morning, I was to help papa with his extra volume of dairy products, demanded by the Thanksgiving holiday weekend.

I remember servicing Mr. Turner's home that memorable Thanksgiving Eve morning. Papa and I had started emptying the little white milk wagon down at Doc Thomas' drugstore - down near Highway '62. The next stop was Mrs. Berry's hotel and cafe, located on the northwest corner of the Masonic Temple.

My fear of not finishing in time to make the trip was beginning to show. Papa insisted on talking at length with a customer or a friendly neighbor on the street. My concerns about the scheduled basketball trip seemed extremely trite and even annoying to my father. For one who had been forced to scuffle for himself as a boy, denied of very little formal education, my obsession to participate in sports was beyond his understanding. He couldn't envision what playing ball, "running around the country - coming back at all hours of the night had to do with my preparation to become a preacher.

I remember my older brother Cleophas, wanted to play football several years before, while he attended Boley High. Papa put an end to that, only after they had a violent quarrel. It wasn't long before Cleophas had quit school and joined my brothers up in Detroit.

It's funny, how when you're young, everything seems to revolve around your personal interests and pursuits alone. I was too busy with my own doings to observe that the whole town, especially the merchants, were uptight about their money in Mr. Turner's bank and Pretty Boy Floyd's gang.

Most of the kids my age could remember too vividly when another brand of law breakers had threatened to march down Boley's main street.

They were the Klu Klux Klan.

They had been turned back two miles east of Boley, near the Sand Creek School. On that night, Marshall John Owens and scores of veterans from

World War 1 had sealed off the town, barricading the highway at the east and west sides of town.

Like the Klan, Pretty Boy usually announced the date he planned to rob a certain town's bank. As yet, Boley had received no such warning.

"Their Home...Their Castle
Bah, bah Black bank!
Have you lots of loot?
Yes sir, and Sheriff Lank and
guns that shoot and shoot..."

For all intent and purposes, Charles Pete Glass, on the day before Thanksgiving, 1932, was a twenty-six-year-old male Caucasian. The night before, he had fraternized with a rather exclusive fraternity of white bank robbers. George Curley Birdwell had taken him in, in spite of Pretty Boy's warning...

"Somebody's liable to get killed in that Nigra town."

Pete Glass thought proudly of himself, in finally being accepted as an equal. Over the years, Glass had visited the girls and gambled in the all-black town as a Negro.

It was eight o'clock in the morning at Earlsboro where Glass and his boss, Birdwell and the Kiowa bandit, C. C. Patterson, were preparing to leave for Boley. They had eaten breakfast, without Pretty Boy, at the farmhouse of Dock Hearn, a black farmer, near Earlsboro.

C. C. Patterson adjusted his shoulder holster, picked up his sawed-off shotgun and walked toward ther black Buick sedan.

"All right! It's time!" Patterson scowled.

"Let's hit, it or forgit it!."

Patterson quickly placed himself in his regular position under the wheel of the car. Although Glass was the new wheel man for the Boley caper, he knew that Patterson would drive the first leg of the trip. Glass and Birdwell entered opposite sides of the car to the back seat. Without Pretty Boy, Glass was engulfed in a strange mixture of fear and excitement. Birdwell, having taken a hefty swig from his bottle, offered it to Glass. He needed a shot – maybe a double, Birdwell thought.

The black sedan growled and spun its wheels into Dock Hearn's reddish dirt and gravel yard. Patterson gunned the accelerator and quickly turned the car toward Okemah. Speculations were that Pretty Boy had plans to make a sneak visit to his ailing wife, reportedly in a hospital at Tulsa, sixty miles north of Boley.

Several miles before reaching Boley, C. C. Patterson relinquished his seat at the wheel to Pete Glass. This was in accordance with the Birdwell plan of attack.

Pete Glass felt somewhat more at ease under

the wheel, in the driver's seat. At last, he was a working part of the operation– a forerunner in this kind of job integration.

By ten-thirty, the black, beetle-shaped Buick was gliding smoothly down black-top highway '62.

George Birdwell and company turned off the highway and onto Boley's Main Street. Bumping over the railroad tracks that ran parallel to the highway, Pete Glass probably wished he was a shade darker in complexion; people on Main Street might perceive him with less suspicion. The unseasonably cold weather had forced Pete to turn up the collar of his top coat. All three men were silent-watching from the corners of their eyes.

Birdwell's instructions were to have Pete park on the wrong side of the street, still headed north, up Main Street. It was only a half hour or so after the bank had opened and very little auto traffic was anywhere in the street. Only a few wagons with farmers moved briskly against the chilly north wind.

Pete pulled the car to the opposite side of the street and grinded to a creeping halt just south of the Farmers and Merchants Bank. Parked in this manner, no one in the bank would be able to see the car of strangers pass the bank to make the usual "U" turn, heading the car back toward the highway. To escape, Pete (the driver) would merely put the car in reverse, back up in a short half-circle, and turn toward the highway and make their get- away.

C. C. Patterson stood briefly adjusting his sawed - off shotgun under his long overcoat. He was soon following Birdwell on the sidewalk leading to the bank's entrance. Pete Glass remained in the car. He watched Birdwell and Patterson enter the bank.

The duo of experienced bank robbers did not arouse the suspicions of W. W. Riley, the bank's treasurer, who was engaged in conversation with a customer named Horace Aldridge. They were near the back of the bank!

No one seemed to notice the manner in which Pete was parked. So far, that was good. He lit a cigarette.

Birdwell walked casually toward the caged teller's window. D. J. Turner saw immediately that the white gentleman wasn't Pretty Boy. Patterson's long coat barely concealed his sawed-off shotgun. Turner, the bank president, serving as teller, smiled and opened his mouth to speak. Suddenly, Birdwell's Army forty-five automatic was pointing straight at Turner's slightly receding hairline.

"We're robbin' this bank!" Birdwell said, in a moderately loud voice and ordered Turner, "Hand over the dough! Don't pull no alarm!"

Upon hearing Birdwell's order, H. C. McCormick, the bank's bookkeeper, slipped to the floor and crawled toward the large vault door. D. J. Turner began calmly pushing the paper money under the cash slot beneath the steel bars of the window. Quickly, most of the bills were pulled from the cash drawer and jammed under the window. The last handful that Turner pulled included the last bill in the drawer.

The two electrodes rigged in the drawer clamped together and the alarm screamed. The same siren alerted the proprietors in four other stores.

By this time, McCormick was on his knees in the man-sized vault. He reached for the rifle that leaned against the inside vault wall and began to crack the vault's big steel gray door open wider.

Birdwell bellowed at the bank president, "You pulled the alarm? I'll kill ya for that, goddamn you!"

Instinctively, Birdwell's hand reached again and grabbed a handful of bills.

D. J. growled, "You bet I pulled it!"

"Don't hurt nobody. Please!" W. W. Riley pleaded to C. C. Patterson, who had raised a sawed-off shotgun from under his overcoat.

"Shut up! You," Patterson yelled.

"Get your hands over your head, nigger!"

Birdwell's finger squeezed the trigger of his .45 Army automatic pistol and Turner's body was blown back toward the desk. He pulled the trigger three more times. The banker's body slumped to the floor. His riddled-body made a loud thump, as he rolled over, clutching the top of his desk.

Birdwell's gun was still smoking, pointing toward the fallen bank president, when McCormick pushed his 20-30 Winchester rifle barrel through the vault door's crack, over its top hinges.

He fired!

Birdwell's heavy forty-five fell and bounced on the hardwood floor beside him. He staggered. Blood spurted from under his chin as he fell.

"I'm shot!" Birdwell hollered.

"Hold me! I'm ..." He rolled over on the floor beside his gun. H. C. McCormick's single shot had entered his neck.

C. C. Patterson waved his sawed-off shotgun menacingly at Riley and the frightened customer. He ordered the two men to pull Birdwell to the outside. They eagerly obeyed, seeing that the bandit already appeared nearly dead.

Pete Glass, responding to the alarm and the shots as a signal of trouble, rushed into the bank with his pistol drawn. While Patterson grabbed at the money that Birdwell had dropped on the floor, Pete was pulling the last bills out of the teller's window, stuffing them in his overcoat pockets.

"Somebody's back there! They shot Curly!"

Patterson told Pete. "We got to get goin.' Let's git out of here!" Patterson yelled.

Pete fired his gun twice, at random, toward the back of the bank and turned to follow the two men dragging Birdwell out the front door. He continued to grab money off the floor and stuff the scattered greenbacks into his overcoat pockets. He scurried toward the front door, then stood briefly in the door and looked up Main Street – listening to the echo of the bank's alarms from the stores along Main Street.

The men he had watched walking briskly before he entered the bank were now running down Main Street toward the bank. Some already carried shotguns and rifles.

"He pulled that god-dammed alarm." Pete breathed, as Riley and Horace Aldridge dumped Birdwell on the sidewalk in front of the bank and scampered around the corner to the side street.

"That crazy old man... pulled that alarm...!" Pete mumbled.

C. C. Patterson bent over to pick up Birdwell, beckoning to Pete to help.

Unexpectedly, Patterson was suddenly hit by a blast of buckshots from behind. It was a man named Zeigler – down behind Lonnie Turner's hardware store. Patterson was so surprised that he yelped like a dog and grabbed his hip and right leg.

Pete, seeing Patterson hit, quickly dived to the

sidewalk, then crawled toward Birdwell –with waning hope to getting him to the car.

Patterson waved his shotgun up at Bill Hazel, who had reached his position on the veranda of his store across the street. Patterson shot, as Bill Hazel ducked behind the railing.

By this time, sheriff Langston McCormick, followed by a platoon of men with rifles, rushed out of the American Legion Hall located in the Masonic Temple. (They had secured guns there.) Crouched with gun in hand, running behind the sheriff to take position on the vacant lot facing the bank, was Raymond Parker, a former Boley High football star.

Now, the battle lines were clearly drawn.

Pete Glass quickly discovered that he and Patterson were trying to save a dead man. Pete rose up, greenbacks sticking grotesquely out of his overcoat pockets, and began running, half bent over. His car was approximately fifty feet south of the bank's front door.

Scores of men were now swarming down Main Street, as if the sidewalks and the dusty street itself had opened up and they emerged from underground. Many were just farmers – in town for their Thanksgiving hunting needs. Bullets screamed and crashed against the bank, through the front window.

Outside on the sidewalks, C. C. Patterson bent over to pull Birdwell by his overcoat collar with his left hand, his right hand holding his sawed-off shotgun.

He was hit again from behind by the same Zeigler. Patterson grabbed at his back and lower extremities and fired at random toward Doc Thomas' pharmacy. Bill Hazel, high above on his veranda, took dead aim with his double-barreled shotgun at Patterson. The shotgun boomed. He missed him.

From across the street, the sheriff along with Raymond Parker, trained their guns on Patterson as he whipped his sawed-off shotgun up and pointed it at Bill Hazel again. Before he could get his shot off, Langston McCormick's and Parker's bullets blew his gun from his hands and dropped him to the sidewalk. He fell behind Birdwell–holding his right shoulder.

Bullets screamed above them - all around them, ricocheting against the front of the bank, spraying it and keeping Herbert McCormick pinned down inside.

Miraculously, Glass succeeded somehow in reaching the black Buick get-away car, without being struck by the volley of bullets that sprayed all around and above him. Immediately, upon gaining entrance to the big Buick, he was facing up Main Street.

Now the horde of vigilante's fire was trained at his face. He had no time to retaliate. He stepped on the starter and began to back up, circling the short turn that quickly made him face back toward the South and the highway.

John Owens, the retired town marshal, who had rushed down Main Street from his store, was nearing the intersection. Seeing the escaping get-away car approximately fifty yards away, Owens dropped to his knees in the middle of Main Street. He rested his rifle on one knee and fired, as Pete went into the short, half turn.

Pete was hit by Owens rifle bullet. The black Buick continued to back up and whirl across and down the opposite side of the street–out of control. When it crashed against the embankment of the vacant lot, the whole town seemed to pour lead into the black, beetle-shaped car.

The car and Pete rocked under the bullets' and buckshot's screaming assault. Soon Pete's head and shoulders were draped over the steering wheel, still facing up Main Street. One of his arms dangled out the window. His brief career in crime had ended.

Sheriff Langston McCormick called out for the men to cease firing. Immediately, some began to run from across the street toward the front of the bank where Patterson lay wounded, but still alive on the sidewalk.

At this moment, Dr. Paxton rushed into the bank carrying his medicine bag and his rifle. W. W.

Riley, the treasurer, had put the word out that Turner was shot. Dr. Paxton hurried into the bank, trailed by the sheriff and several others. Herbert McCormick was found kneeling on the floor beside his bullet-riddled boss, Dave Turner. Turner was barely conscious.

Some of the men were thoroughly angered and enraged when they learned that Turner was shot. Others yelled, "We got 'em, we got Pretty Boy!"

Angry blood-thirsty voices shouting in the crowd of vigilantes now were calling for revenge for those who had shot Turner.

"Give me a piece of the one with the shotgun! He ain't dead! Let's finish him!"

Lank McCormick returned from the bank, upon hearing the highly incensed voices outside. Dr. Paxton had told him that the bank president wasn't dead. Lank moved through the crowd swiftly, his tall figure booming out orders. His brother Herbert, who was outside now, joined the angry vigilantes with their shouts and demands for revenge for Turner's critical condition.

They wanted the wounded Patterson dead. Marshall Lank McCormick moved in quickly to console the crowd.

"All right now, that's enough of that talk. Doc says D. J. is hanging on. He's still alive."

He moved in front of Herbert, still trying to

calm him down. When his brother was stubbornly restrained, Lank raised his Winchester over his head and pushed the crowd back from the fallen bandits, barking out orders to the men to "step back!" "Now, I don't stand for no different treatment" Lank announced. "He's my prisoner. Now y'all back off!"

"Which one's Pretty Boy?" somebody hollered.

"Neither one, I don't reckon," Lank answered.

He bent over to ask the badly wounded Patterson about Pretty Boy. After a moment, he turned to the crowd and spoke. "He says Pretty Boy didn't come. Birdwell's the dead one."

The crowd was stunned-disappointed that they had captured anybody less than the terror of the plains, Pretty Boy Floyd.

Dr. Paxton had quickly decided to move Turner to the hospital in Okemah as soon as possible. The doctor followed closely behind his semi-conscious friend as he was carried from the bank. He glanced briefly at C. C. Patterson's blood-spattered form on the ground and hurried behind Bill Hazel, who was already waiting with his car out front. One man called out to the doctor.

"You sure they goin' take him in the hospital Doc?"

"Maybe not yesterday," the doctor said, "but

they'll take him today. They better!"

Just as Hazel's car was ready to pull off for Olemah, Mrs. Grace Turner, who had heard of the robbery, drove up in her husband's car. She parked quickly and ran toward the car carrying her husband. Dr. Paxton helped her into Bill Hazel's car. She sat propped on her knees holding the banker's head in the back seat. With the doctor's help, she finally was seated with her husband's head cradled in her lap. The doctor motioned Hazel to hurry.

Grace Turner began to talk to Dr. Paxton, holding back her tears. "Just this morning, at the breakfast table," she confided, "he told me he'd have to go back to that 'trap.' I didn't know what he meant... I guess I know what he meant, now. He meant he'd die, springing the trap set for that Pretty Boy –with that alarm. He had a premonition... Lord... my poor Joe."

"Look like it wasn't even Pretty Boy, neither," Doc Paxton informed her. "That damn trigger happy Birdwell."

Hazel's foot was touching the floor board. The speedometer read seventy-five.

They were nearly to Okemah. Grace Turner stared tear-filled eyes at her husband's eyes that would not close.

Dr. Paxton saw his friend was not alive.

He quickly searched his pockets for a white

handkerchief, to cover the dead banker's face.

"We'd better stop," the doctor said to Bill Hazel. "He's gone."

Hazel cruised to a silent halt on the highway. Dr. Paxton was soon closing D. J. Turner's eyes.

The minute Papa and I had finished delivering the town's fresh milk supply, I was dropped off at Boley High. By that time, the shocking news of Mr. Turner being shot by the Floyd gang was all over town.

The two cars carrying the basketball team to Wewoka were soon cruising down Main Street toward Highway '62. When we passed the bank the coach refused to let us stop. We did have a long trip ahead of us.

I remembered the three bodies covered with sheets, lying in front of the bank as we passed by. Everyone in my car was sure one of the dead men under the sheets was Pretty Boy Floyd. A huge crowd had gathered. Everybody was waiting for the ambulance from Okemah.

As I left that bizarre scene, I found both emotions of sadness and excitement in turmoil within me. Before we reached the highway, a strong surge of pride was lodged in my throat.

My team-mates kept yelling,

"They got Pretty Boy!

They got Pretty Boy!

They killed the No. 1 Enemy! No more robbin' for Robin Hood!"

Victory that afternoon at Wewoka was inevitable. The five guys most responsible for it were: Clifford "Chick" Owens, Millard Brooks, Luther Woodward, Steve and Otis Johnson.

The ambulance from Okemah picked up the three bandits and delivered two of them to the county morgue. C. C. Patterson was hospitalized with two serious gunshot wounds. His back, legs and posterior were a seed-bed of buckshots. Doctors at Okemah worked for hours digging them out.

The day after the foiled bank robbery at Boley, the Daily Oklahoman newspaper carried the following report, identifying the members of Pretty Boy Floyd's gang that bit the dust at Boley.

"Patterson, who was unable to speak because of bullet wounds in the neck, confirmed that the dead bandit was Birdwell by nodding his head to A. B. Cooper, the agency operative of the W. J. Burns International Detective Agency.

Positive identification of George Birdwell, notorious lieutenant of Pretty Boy Floyd, Oklahoma desperado, as one of the bandits killed in the attempted robbery of the Farmers and Merchants Bank at Boley, Negro city, was made Wednesday night by Charles Dore, Seminole county deputy sheriff.

Known to be the lieutenant of Floyd, Birdwell shared the notorious outlaw's reputation.

For months he had been sought by police of half dozen state's cities charged in connection with bank robberies, and in several instances, with murder.

Birdwell was considered by police all over the state as the "brains" and the killer of the Floyd-Birdwell combination."

"He is the man who planned these activities and handled the machine gun in their raids," Burns said. (End of quote).

On the cold and misty Saturday afternoon following the bank robbery, a few dozen curious spectators and Pretty Boy Floyd fans viewed Curley Birdwell's remains at the funeral home in Earlsboro. Lurking among the crowd were local police, state police and a couple of FBI men. They were all looking for Pretty Boy, Public Enemy No. 1.

He'd eluded them again, failing to pay his respects to his slain, stubborn little lieutenant. Pretty Boy, later that year, left the state – never to return again to haunt the Oklahoma banks.

Two years later, (1934) Charles A. Pretty Boy Floyd joined his fellow gang members in death. The elusive Sage Brush Robin Hood was cut down by a volley of FBI guns in a desolate corn field in Ohio.

CHAPTER 11
"The Dead Hero"

On Monday, November 28, 1932, approximately five thousand souls lined Pecan Street, (Main) in Boley, Oklahoma to view the funeral procession and pay their last respects to the slain heroic, black banker, David Joseph Turner.

Since early that morning, the stunned mourners and visiting spectators from far and wide had been congregating on Main Street's narrow sidewalks. They stretched in patches from the bullet-riddled bank building to the site of the funeral, six blocks north at the Antioch Baptist Church.

Four days earlier, on November 24, 1932, the Daily Oklahoma newspaper at Oklahoma City, Oklahoma carried the following banner headlines:

"BIRDWELL, AID TO FLOYD DIES
IN BOLEY RAID
Peace Officer Identifies Notorious Outlaw
As Gun Victim.
NEGRO IS HERO
Bank President, Two Bandits Dead,
Third Robber Wounded."

Roscoe D. Dungee's Black Dispatch newspaper,

(published in Oklahoma City) carried the following report:

> "Indians, with their bright colored blankets, old men, tottering with age, formed small clusters telling, in their own particular way, how David Turner, the daddy of Boley, had in some way helped them, or in some way inspired them to help themselves."

A white spokesman from the Oklahoma Banker's Association eulogized at the funeral serv-ices with moving words of praise. He compared Boley as: "A shooting star, rising over a troubled and uncharted wilderness, with D. J. Turner as the star's guiding pilot on its bright journey across a checkerboard of whites, Negroes and Indians."

A truckload of flowers led the procession from the church to the burial grounds. Notable citizens, black and white, were represented from distant cities in Oklahoma. Intermingled in the crowd were the Boley vigilantes, who had then arrived with Sheriff Langston McCormick in the nick of time to help protect the nation's only black-owned and operated bank.

My father and I were among those paying their respects to D. J., as he was affectionately called. The broad cross-section of mourners at Boley's biggest funeral was a living testimony that the Floyd myth (the Robin Hood syndrome) had died with Birdwell and the remains of Pretty Boy Floyd's gang in the shoot-out.

CHAPTER 12
Backlash for a second hero

The funeral services for the slain Boley hero, the banker D. J. Turner, had naturally upstaged the town's second hero. He was of course, George Birdwell's daring killer, Herbert C. McCormick.

For two weeks, the letters of condolence flowed into the banker's widow's home on Main Street, the mayor's office, and even the sheriff's office. However, the mild-mannered bookkeeper who had cut the boastful Birdwell down, was ironically Boley's first real live hero.

Herbert McCormick took his meteoric ascension to state-wide fame with humility. He was somewhat surprised at the numerous letters and notes of praise from throughout the state. The police and elected officials at Okemah were high in their praise of the sheriff, Herbert's brother. They congratulated him on a "job well done."

Moreover, it was the "hate" letters that arrived from Pretty Boy's followers that pinched the sharp-shooting hero's sensibilities. The dozens of derogatory letters received at the dead banker's office, and by the sheriff were expected. The threatening letters soon narrowed from broad accusations to Birdwell's killer, personally. Four days after the foiled bank robbery attempt, H. C. McCormick received a note addressed to him. It read: "The man who killed my buddy Birdwell, won't live to see Christmas." The letter was signed *Charles "Pretty Boy" Floyd.*

Herbert McCormick thought about his four children and refused to accept the threat as an hoax. There were four McCormick brothers at Boley. None could ever be accused of running away from a fight. Of the four, Herbert was considered the most gentle in nature. Nonetheless, Herbert began wearing the forty-five Army automatic pistol that Birdwell left behind.

A volunteer group of close friends and relatives began a twenty-four hour vigil in the close vicinity of the book-keeper's home. Christmas was more than three weeks away. Instead of hero, Herbert was literally more of a prisoner in his own heroism.

For many years, the standing reward given by the State of Oklahoma for "Killing a man in the act of robbing a bank" was $250.00. This was a far cry from the $6,000.00 that still hung over the elusive Pretty Boy Floyd's head. However, the paltry sum would be eagerly received by Herbert C. McCormick. According to his wife, Abigail, the mild-mannered Sunday school superintendent, received an additional $1,000.00 from the Oklahoma Bankers Association.

Several weeks after the foiled bank robbery attempt, Herbert C. McCormick defied the backlash of threats on his life and motored to the State Capitol at Oklahoma to receive his reward from Governor William "Alfalfa" Bill Murray.

Driving through Oklahoma City to the Capitol Building, all eyes scanned the oil derricks that rose up from the back yards of many residential homes. In contrast to the sound of pumping oil derricks were the long lines of the poor. Hordes of men stood bewildered, waiting at relief stations for a bowl of soup to warm their insides.

Noticeably, the oil rich, local Indians whizzed by in their long limousines, dressed in full Indian headdresses and cowboy boots.

Soon, the imposing, alabaster columns that fronted the capitol building loomed before the Boley hero. Huge oil derricks stood on the grounds of the capitol building site. Herbert, like most Sooners, had read about the wildcat digging and discovery of oil on the Capitol grounds only a few years before. Sheriff Langston McCormick remembered his dual purpose for being with his brother and remained just outside the governor's suite.

As he drove along, Herbert watched intently

for shady-looking characters bent on revenging Birdwell's death.

Facing Governor Bill Murray to receive the reward, Herbert McCormick felt at ease and satisfied with himself. He was lucky. He thought about his home-town vigilantes and his brother, who would love to be in his shoes. His town's overwhelming victory over three fourths of the legendary Floyd's gang had precipitated a mite of luster to his home town's name, literally putting it on the map.

Herbert McCormick stood erect. A glimmer of a smile illuminated his wife, Abigale's face, when the governor presented him the $250.00 check. Upon congratulating him, the governor remarked that he had "kept his head, in the face of danger." In addition to the cash award, the governor, who had campaigned for governor in an Old model T Ford, bestowed upon him the honorary title of "Major," for as long as he should live. Major McCormick lived thirty five more years, serving his state in various official capacities. A fluke of fate, shrouded in irony was to eventually contribute to his demise in 1967.

Many years after the bank shoot-out, George Birdwell's revolver, that the Major had kept as a souvenir, discharged accidentally, tearing into his leg. The wound that was inflicted never healed properly. The tragic incident was to contribute heavily to his demise

EPILOUGE

Near the middle of May in the year 1933, most of Boley's residents had turned out at the gym at Boley High to hear the principal speaker for the graduation day exercise of the "Class of '33."

The mid-day sun squeezed warm sheaths of light through the school's tall gymnasium windows. The gym, now converted into a chapel, gave the appearance of the interior of a church. Among those seniors who graced the small platform stage was Leon Eugene Smith. Colonel Smith's youngest boy was well known to most of the audience, not for basketball, but for his acting performances on the small stage where he was seated.

The young Smith's budding talent had been discovered a year earlier in his portrayal of the Japanese butler in the three-act play, "The Bat"– with Cleo Johnson. As a senior, he starred (opposite Lerline George) in the operetta, "Tulip Time in Holland."

Moreover, at the graduation ceremonies, he was to rise and receive a moment's recognition as class poet and contributor of the class motto. The motto was: "On Our Own Wings We Strive to Climb."

The following Fall (1933), he received a room

and board scholarship to Wiley College. Most of the $125.00 tuition was paid with the money he earned from the sale of one bale of cotton from my second cotton patch.

Among his few graduation gifts were two small bibles and a 'BOLEY BEARS' basketball sweater - with a big "B" blazing in front.

Although our town was struggling to survive the continued impact of the Great Depression and the loss of its political and financial leader, D. J. Turner, nearly half of his class were going off to college. It wasn't long before the Farmers and Merchants Bank re-opened its doors (1935).

Boley 's new bank president's name was M. W. Lee. He served the town for many years, contributing much to its economic growth. Today, his son who followed in his father's footsteps at Boley, is a successful entrepreneur in an enterprise established by his late father.

Boley will always be a symbol of man's will power and "can do."

Long Live That Bullish Boley Spirit!